HUNGER IN THE HEART OF GOD

Hunger in the Heart of God

New Hope for a Hurting World

Ted W. Engstrom
with
Robert C. Larson

VINE
BOOKS

Servant Publications
Ann Arbor, Michigan

Copyright © 1989 Ted W. Engstrom and Robert C. Larson
Assoc., Inc.

Vine Books is an imprint of Servant Publications especially
designed to serve Evangelical Christians.

The Bible texts in this publication is from *The New King James
Bible*. Copyright © 1979, 1980, 1982, Thomas Nelson Inc.,
Publishers.

Published by Servant Books
P.O. Box 8617
Ann Arbor, Michigan 48107

Cover design by Charles Piccirillo & Bob Coe
Cover photo by Lawrence Fitton

89 90 91 92 93 94 10 9 8 7 6 5 4 3 2 1

Printed in the United States of America
ISBN 0-89283-622-9

Library of Congress Cataloging-in-Publication Data

Engstrom, Theodore Wilhelm, 1916-
  Hunger in the heart of God : hope for a hurting world / by
Ted Engstrom and Bob Larson.
    p. cm.
  Bibliography : p.
  ISBN 0-89283-622-9
  1. God—Love. 2. God—Worship and love. 3. Love—
Religious aspects—Christianity. 4. Hunger—Religious
aspects—Christianity. I. Larson, Bob. II. Title.
BT140.E54   1989
261.8—dc19   89-30989
                                                   CIP

Contents

Introduction

TWO ELEMENTS COMBINED MAKE A CARPET or tapestry strong: *warp and woof.* Each has its own function. Neither can survive without the other. Likewise, in coming to an understanding of the explosive issues relating to world hunger there are also two elements which must be interlinked or we risk presenting little more than half-truths. These two components are the irrefutable facts of hunger and the changeless truth of the gospel.

Early on we hope you'll discover these pages are not a mere recitation of more shop-worn facts regarding hunger. But there are facts. Nor is the book our attempt to promulgate a theology of hunger, as useful as that discussion might be. However, we do quote freely and boldly from Scripture as we feel it relates to the subject at hand.

In essence, what we have tried to do in this volume is provide you a vital, even obligatory, warp and woof regarding hunger in all its aspects. The warp is the physical need all humans have for nutritious food and sustenance; the woof is that seemingly insatiable hunger that exists in the heart of a loving God . . . a hunger and a hope that his sons and daughters will be more considerate, caring, and compassionate toward the multifaceted needs—emotional, physical, social, and spiritual—of his suffering creation.

To come to the point: if your heart is moved by a hungry, hurting planet and you choose to be more effective in your personal response, this book is for you. On the other hand, if you are interested in engaging God in a one-to-one dialogue about the hunger he might have in his caring heart, then this book is also for you. We hope you will be concerned with both.

It is our prayer that *Hunger in the Heart of God* will persuade you to apply your Christian faith to real life situations in a way that perhaps you have never done before. We hope this book will encourage you to extend yourself even further to assist the sick, the hungry, the lonely, the homeless, and the disen-franchised. As you do, we pray God will also create a renewed hunger in your own heart for what he wants most from his creation—an ever diligent quest for personal integrity, truth, and righteousness.

Thank you for taking the time to read these pages.

If what follows encourages you to think more deeply about physical and spiritual hunger, about a loving and almighty God, and about your personal, prayerful response to human need wherever it exists, then our purpose in writing this book will have been served.

Ted W. Engstrom and
Robert C. Larson

"How in the world do I dare eat this good meal in Paris while that mother in Ghana doesn't have enough food to keep her baby alive?" The rest of that pizza might have been greasy cardboard for all the appeal it offered me now.

Accepting the Unacceptable

The WORTHY FOUNDATION
Cordially invites you to join
a Stunning Movie Star
the Top Politician
and a Leading Business Tycoon
for a Surprise Banquet
of International Cuisine
to help relieve world hunger.
RSVP
(Large Sum) per plate

(Imagine the names of your favorite, "irresistible" celebrities.)

YOU DECIDE TO ATTEND THE OCCASION and look forward to the evening with delight. Here's your opportunity to rub shoulders with some of the leading citizens in your community, to say nothing of the VIPs. The fact that it's supporting a worthy cause makes it a bit easier to endure the lofty ticket price.

On the night of the banquet, you and your escort dress up in the finest "black tie" attire in town. Whom will you meet? What will they serve? Who will speak?

"I'm so glad you could join us," beams one of the Foundation hosts you recognize. "Please help yourself to the bar for some juice or ice water."

"Juice? Ice water?" you silently repeat in your mind. "Where are the cocktails?"

"Hors d'oeuvres, anyone?" chimes a waitress. There on a lovely serving tray are carrot twirls, broccoli heads, cauliflower slices, celery, mushrooms, and other raw vegetables with no sauce or dip.

"No thanks," you reply, casting an eye for some canapes or meat appetizers. "Are there any other choices?" you allow to slip from your lips.

"No, this is our full selection," replies the waitress with only the slightest hint of apology.

Now you're beginning to feel concerned that you allowed yourself to get hungry before this banquet. Every other occasion you've attended or heard about in this dining room offered the richest spread around. Maybe the main course will be more promising.

Others are talking politely and comparing beverages with one another in a somewhat skeptical manner. The spartan offerings lend themselves to a discussion of the main purpose of the event, world hunger. Could it be the hosts have a more personal message to convey this evening?

You make your way into the banquet hall and find your name on a card placed next to a leading personality from the community. Salads are already in place, but they look rather plain. In fact, the tired old joke about "honeymoon salad" comes to mind because they are "lettuce alone." But because it's so old and tiresome you don't bother to tell it.

"Ladies and gentlemen, please find your places," calls out one of the hosts. "We're about ready to begin our meal. You're probably wondering what's on the menu after our unique cocktails and appetizers. Welcome to a 'world meal for world relief,' " he continues. "You have your choice of fish or chicken served on a bed of rice. The choice of beverage is water and tea."

Audible sighs and groans ripple through the banquet hall.

"This meal approximates what the average world citizen eats. Except our choice tonight is somewhat wider and the portions are larger for this festive occasion. We felt it was a fitting gesture to our brothers around the world to face this pressing issue from a similar point of view. Please enjoy your meal. The amounts we have allocated for the 500 of us tonight could feed 2500 or more people in Africa, South America, or Asia."

You nibble your salad feeling more like a rabbit than a contributor. Mercifully, the hosts have provided small bottles of oil and vinegar dressing to give it some taste.

"Chicken or fish?" inquires the waiter. You glance across at another table already being served and notice it doesn't really make much difference. The portion of meat on the plates is too small to distinguish whether it's fish or fowl alongside the modest mound of rice. "Either one," you shrug.

Conversations are hushed and barely slice their way through the aroma of steamed fish, chicken, and rice. There isn't much to say. Only a world of meaning to imbibe.

"Maybe 48 Hours"

I remember so well the case of one young mother who quite likely would have given all she owned to partake of such a "banquet."

It was a few years ago in Ghana. I was walking through a relief camp and saw a distraught mother. She had a four-year-old alongside and a tiny baby in her arms. She was poorly clothed and extremely thin. I stopped with a nurse and Director Commodore Quaye, my interpreter, and began to talk with the young lady.

"Where's your husband? Is he out in the field?"

"No," she replied through the interpreter. "He died a couple of months ago."

"What happened?" I inquired.

"Well, he didn't have enough to feed himself. He fed us but he couldn't feed himself."

"How old is your baby?"

"Four months, I think."

"Boy or girl?"

"She's a girl."

"Well, I love little children. May I please hold her?"

She passed the child over to me and what I felt made me instantly ill. The child was nothing more than skin and bones—a bundle of broom sticks wrapped in a sickly parchment that passed for flesh. No muscle, no tissue. Only dry skin, vacant eyes, and fragile bones.

I held that child for a while and the nurse came over to examine her. She put the stethoscope to the little one's heart and said, "This child won't survive any more than 24, maybe 48 hours."

"Well, she must survive," I said as if coming in contact with me was some sort of healing shadow. "Can't the mother feed her?"

"No, she has no milk at all."

"Well, we have gruel here in the camp to feed other children. Can't we feed this baby?" (Gruel is warm cereal made from fafa, a soy-wheat combination with a little sugar, oil, and dried skim milk.)

"No, I'm sorry. She's too far gone. She can't contain any food," said the nurse in what amounted to a death sentence.

I swallowed hard and gently gave the child back to her mother and a part of myself along with her. I was angry, frustrated, and sad. But we had to continue our tour of the facility. By that evening I found myself back in the capital of Accra boarding a late night flight to Paris.

It's astounding what a few hours and a few thousand miles will do for one's perception. The next day a colleague of mine, Ralph Sanford, and I had gone out shopping and later tried some pizza—Paris style. But after two bites, I began to choke on the brutal realization, "How in the world do I dare eat this good meal in Paris while that mother in Ghana doesn't have enough food to keep her baby alive?" The rest of that pizza might as well have been greasy cardboard for all the appeal it offered me now.

That mother, her martyred husband, and her slowly dying infant are typical of millions of families all over the world who simply don't have enough food to eat. I had a deep problem with that reality. Being out in the field with people who are hungry—both physically and spiritually—normally doesn't destroy me. I've had to learn to cope with the trauma. That's part of what I choose to see. I've done that for a quarter of a century now. My problem has always been coming back to our affluent, wasteful, arrogant society and trying to adjust to a lifestyle that's so foreign to what the rest of the world endures. That's where I struggle, and that's where every thinking person—such as you, my reader friend—may be struggling as well. But don't leave me. Be my companion as I struggle through these pages.

A World Denied

According to Arthur Simon, president of Bread for the World, a Washington-based citizens' congress, almost one billion people live in absolute poverty. They do not have enough food. They have no clean water. Essential health services are unheard of. According to the United Nations, forty thousand young children die from malnutrition and disease *every day*. 40,000! Yet every year the nations of the world spend in excess of 950 billion dollars for weapons that destroy. This, according to Mr. Simon, represents more than three times the total annual income of the poorest billion people on earth.[1]

How dare we accept such unacceptable conditions? Could it be we're . . .

Happy with Hunger

Could it be that too many well-fed people in the West are strangely content as long as hunger's victims suffer politely out of sight and out of mind? After all, "Someone else is taking care of them, aren't they? Well, aren't they?"

Based on years of firsthand experience as a social worker, one Christian author said:

> There seems to be within the American psyche a deep animosity towards our poor. We find greater tolerance in our hearts for the Mafia and for those involved in white-collar crime—after all, they keep their yards up and they're obviously successful in their work—but we hate the welfare mother who is struggling to simply keep life together.[2]

Those in the country of my birth, the United States, have no monopoly on this unappetizing prejudice. I've heard it expressed in Canada, London, France, Germany, Switzerland, South Africa—spoken quietly wherever the "haves" realize they have nothing to gain from the "have-nots."

To uninformed and out of touch observers, the victims of malnutrition often appear to be "happy with hunger" because of the jubilation they exhibit upon receiving the bags full of rice or flour—enough to last a few hours or days (often at less than subsistence levels). However, when this temporary satisfaction wears off, the hungry have neither the strength, knowledge, or resources to improve their long term condition.

Dictators and revolutionaries are often "happy with hunger" because they can use it as yet another weapon in their deadly arsenal. For example, civil war has raged in Ethiopia for nearly thirty years. Recently the Tigray People's Liberation Front (TPLF) started launching new raids that effectively cut off nearly all supplies to distribution centers providing food for some 550,000 people. *US News and World Report* said this "controlled famine" poses new threats of starvation for a million or more people caught in a sudden escalation of this bitter civil war. Glad perpetrators create sad victims.[3]

This diet of destruction repeats itself every day throughout the world. Lebanon, the West Bank, Angola, Central America, Afghanistan, Nicaragua, Northern Ireland are but a few of the international hot spots which happily seem to dish out food as a weapon.

Of every one hundred babies born in the world, forty will die before the age of six. Another forty risk permanent physical and mental damage because of malnutrition. Only three out of that hundred will get education and skills they need to perform creative and meaningful work.[4]

Promise of Famine?

Must we continue to accept the unacceptable? Some may have been confused by passages from the Bible which suggest famine and hunger are prime requisites before the return of Christ. Others lean on the statement by Jesus, "The poor you will always have with you," as a reason for global inaction. What is the proper perspective?

A formal study of the "end-time" certainly recognizes the existence of famine before the return of Christ. There's no disputing when the disciples wanted to know, "What will be the sign of Your coming, and of the end of the age?" Christ included in his answer, "There will be famines, pestilences, and earthquakes in various places" (Mt 24:3, 7).

Further, the Book of Revelation mentions scarcity and deadly famine in two of its famed "seven seals" which are opened before the return of Christ.

I looked, and behold, a black horse, and he who sat on it had a pair of scales in his hand. And I heard a voice in the midst of the four living creatures saying, "A quart of wheat for a denarius (about a day's wage), and three quarts of barley for a denarius; and do not harm the oil and the wine."

When He opened the fourth seal, I heard the voice of the fourth living creature saying, "Come and see." And I looked, and behold, a pale horse. And the name of him who sat on it was Death, and Hades followed with him. And power was given to them over a fourth of the earth, to kill with sword, with hunger, with death, and by the beasts of the earth. (Rv 6:5-8)

But are such passages a license for any one of us to ignore the pressing needs of our brothers and sisters in the two-thirds world? From my perspective as a world traveler who has sought to do his best to help alleviate suffering on every inhabitable continent, I'm convinced the family of man has experienced enough famine and hunger to satisfy these prophecies many times over. Now—and more than ever before—rather than sitting back and waiting for things to get worse before praying, "Thy Kingdom come," I'm inclined to praise God for the accuracy of his Word and press forward as a faithful servant, "whom his master will find so doing when he comes" (Lk 12:43).

This ride across the pages of Revelation is not said to be the judgment of God upon the earth. The black horseman's ravages are the work of man upon himself. Having sown the wind, man reaps the whirlwind. It is one of God's laws, built into the very fabric of creation.

"You Have the Poor with You Always"

What about that statement from Christ, "For you have the poor with you always" (Mt 26:11)? Doesn't that mean we should let these unfortunate victims somehow fend for themselves or get by with whatever social programs may be available at the time?

I really don't think so. And I have a sense *you don't either!* Christ made that statement during the week of his crucifixion. Mary, the sister of Martha and Lazarus, had come to honor the Master by anointing him with costly oil as a sign of respect at his death and burial. But this offer of respect offended Judas, who had other designs for the money. "Why was this fragrant oil not sold for three hundred denarii and given to the poor?" (Jn 12:5).

Did Judas, the traitor, have more concern for the poor than our Savior? "This he said, not that he cared for the poor, but because he was a thief, and had the money box; and used to take what was put in it" (Jn 12:6).

It was at this point Christ said, "Let her alone; she has kept this for the day of My burial. For the poor you have with you always, but Me you do not have always" (Jn 12:7-8).

To my layman's way of thinking that oil *was* being used *for the unfortunate and downtrodden.* That evening, Christ himself was numbered among the poorest of the poor. Betrayed by one of his best friends. Arrested on false charges. Tried illegally by his own people and the all-powerful government of Rome. Stripped of his possessions. Scourged. Sent to die as one "numbered among the transgressors." Forsaken by God the Father. Who has ever been in greater physical or spiritual need? Figuratively and literally, this one who was "poor in spirit" is "with us always" as a lasting memorial to the consequences of sin and the justice of God.

Even laying aside the symbolism of the occasion, this command by Christ in no way diminishes our need to reach out to the poor. On the contrary, this passage reinforces our obligation to serve the needy. Jesus' admonition to focus on his own needs instead of those of the poor was an extremely short-lived request. "Me you do not have always" was only a reminder that his crucifixion was near. That condition would be temporary. It would last only three days and three nights. After such time he had promised to rise from the dead and work with them once again (Mt 16:21).

After seventy-two hours Christ was back with the disciples where he helped them refocus their attention on serving mankind with even greater power and conviction. In fact, this very passage which supposedly tells people not to show concern for the poor contains an invitation to do just the opposite. From the Gospel of Mark we read, "For you have the poor with you always, and *whenever you wish you may do them good*" (Mk 14:7). Once the resurrected Christ was back with his followers, you can be sure he gave them plenty of instruction about doing good to the poor.

The Gospel of John records Christ's final three-fold reminder to Peter to "feed my sheep" (Jn 21:15-17). Yes, he wanted the disciples to feed his followers on the Word of God. But how can a minister feed someone's mind if that person's body is weak and dull from malnutrition?

From the earliest days of the New Testament church, the disciples set their hand to making sure new Christians had enough to eat. None lacked because they shared all things in common during those early days at Jerusalem (Acts 4:32-34). The first deacons were ordained to help streamline a "daily distribution" to widows (Acts 6:1). And Paul seemed to devote a great deal of time and energy toward collecting food stuffs from the Gentiles to relieve the famine which burdened the Jewish Christians in Jerusalem (1 Cor 16:1-3).

From the earliest days, the act of relieving human hunger has played a vital role in the Christian's life. The true believer has never been allowed to accept the unacceptable. Not then. Not now. Not ever!

I Have Not Seen the Righteous Forsaken

David observed, "I have not seen the righteous forsaken, Or his descendants begging bread" (Ps 37:25, NASB). But I have seen them go hungry in country after country. Is God's Word broken? Or is there something more we need to understand about righteousness and "asking" for bread? Moses was righteous in God's eyes, yet he twice endured the hunger of a fast for forty days and forty nights. His followers were often unrighteous and God supplied them with abundant bread in the wilderness. (But they didn't recognize it at first and even called its name manna, literally, "what's this?") Christ, Peter, Paul, and most of the New Testament disciples were often hungry, but never forsaken. When they reached the state where they needed to "pray" fervently for their daily bread, they usually wound up with enough to share with even the unbelievers.

God's ways are far beyond our imagining. We'll see some of these mysteries unveiled in forthcoming pages, where you'll meet a number of down-to-earth people who have learned some lofty lessons through hunger.

The Greater Hunger

But this is only physical hunger. What about the spiritual hunger that underlies this condition? Just as people have reached an uneasy state of happiness with literal hunger, the average westerner seems to be happy with a life of spiritual hunger. The society-destroying problems of substance abuse, crime, family disintegration, and endless moral decay seem lost in a short-term binge of personal satisfaction.

Is it because we in the West have no appetite for managing and sharing our wealth that our nations try to dull their minds through drugs and alcohol? These addictions have been called a "national emergency" by responsible thinkers in Europe and America.

Are we so hungry for cold impersonal "things" that our well-to-do nations have bred a generation of criminals who take without feeling?

Are we so starved for affection that we abuse the very

members of our family who could provide this ingredient—simply because they too hunger for acceptance and affection?

I'm convinced that Western society in particular is locked in the vice-grip of a massive spiritual hunger; one even greater than the physical gnawing that threatens so many. Where only one-fifth of the world's population is languishing in physical hunger, I see the *whole world* in deception by "that serpent of old, called the Devil and Satan, *who deceives the whole world*" (Rv 12:9). I'm not saying there are no Christians. But I am saying that unbeliever and Christian alike are being attacked by this master of delusion. And all too often, he leaves us cold and hungry in the sight of God.

Hunger in the Heart of God

What kind of stomach does God have for hunger? What kind of emptiness does he seek to fill?

You and I hunger for knowledge, so we read. We have a hunger for experience, so we travel. We hunger for entertainment, so we go to movies, plays, and concerts.

What kind of hunger does God feel in *his* heart? Perhaps we can gain some insight from an obituary which was sent to the popular newspaper columnist, Ann Landers. At the time she released this story for her nationwide audience, thirty-seven readers near Seattle had already sent in copies of the same article. It touched a sensitive nerve.

Obituary

Born June 22, 1959, in Seattle, died February 17, 1988, of cardiac arrest due to cocaine abuse. She was a beautiful young woman with strawberry blond curls, a gentle soul and a generous heart. She loved music and backgammon and all growing things, especially roses. She was a gifted writer whose work, known only to a few, showed insight and sensitivity. She died a victim of poverty and drugs—each undermining her ability to fight the other. The lesson of her life is this: If you know someone who is hurting, reach out to that person today; if you are hurting yourself, ask for help. Debbie leaves behind a grieving family, her mother, Mary; her brothers, John, Michael and Gregory; her sisters, Cassandra, Pamela, Linda and Marilee; six nephews and nieces; her partner, Michael, and numerous friends. A private memorial service will be held after cremation.[5]

Like the bereaved author of this obituary, perhaps God is hungering for the opportunity to help those in need. Maybe he's hungering for fellowship, hungering for a response from you, from me, hungering for adoration, hungering for obedience.
We can understand the hunger in the heart of God by looking at the appetites he places in the heart of his people. Consider this telling passage:

> [Jesus said . . .] "Then the King will say to those on His right hand, 'Come, you blessed of My Father, inherit the kingdom prepared for you from the foundation of the world: for I was hungry and you gave Me food; I was thirsty and you gave Me drink; I was a stranger and you took Me in; I was naked and you clothed Me; I was sick and you visited Me; I was in prison and you came to Me.' Then the righteous will answer Him, saying, 'Lord, when did we see You hungry and feed You, or thirsty and give You drink? When did we see You a stranger and take You in, or naked and clothe You? Or when did we see You sick, or in prison, and come to see You?' And the King will answer and say to them, 'Assuredly, I say to you, inasmuch as you have done it to one of the least of these My brethren, you did it to Me.'" (Mt 25:34-40)

One theme we'll see over and over again in this book is *God's hunger for adoration from his people in the form of service to one another*. Jesus said:

"A new commandment I give to you, that you love one another; as I have loved you, that you also love one another. By this all will know that you are My disciples, if you have *love for one another.*" (Jn 13:34, 35)

My wife, Dorothy, and I have two delightful neighbors. We had them over for coffee a few weeks ago. We started talking about friendship and how vital it is for survival and emotional growth. The man said, "We don't have friends." He's a busy real estate executive. His wife works as a salesperson. They were so pleased to be able to come over and have coffee with us. Here is a couple of considerable means that had just confessed a deep, penetrating loneliness.

If people are lonely and want help, they need to find someone—perhaps *you*—to minister to them. They need someone they can identify with, open up to and talk to as an individual. I don't think they need a professional counselor at this point, but rather simply a responsible, warmhearted, loving, caring Christian who will listen, and lead them toward Scripture and prayer.

The French philosopher Blaise Pascal said that there's a *God-shaped vacuum in every human being.* It would seem our job is to feed and nourish that vacuum until the image of Christ is formed within us.

Impoverished people of our world know they hunger for physical nourishment. But that only hides their deeper hungers. They don't feel their hunger for fellowship. They don't understand their intellectual hunger. They don't appreciate their hunger for culture and refinement. They don't praise their hunger for God.

The skid row derelict, the bag lady, the child of a cardboard berth cannot comprehend the greatest hunger of all—the hunger of God for his potential sons and daughters.

Can you?

Our next chapter outlines the scope of this world's physical hunger and provides us with a glimpse at its spiritual implications for you as an individual.

There are enough resources in the world to support a decent life for the predicted global population of the year 2000, but not to support lopsided opulence or continual ecological plunder.

TWO

The Inverted Cornucopia

JUST ABOUT EVERYONE IS FAMILIAR with a cornucopia. This symbolic "horn of plenty" represents abundance and material well-being. You see it filled with fruits and grains to the point of overflow. America, along with most of the western world, easily identifies with this symbol of abundance. But for the rest of the world it might have more meaning were it to be hung upside down and empty. "Copia" comes from the same Latin word as "copious" or plentiful. But that assessment doesn't match what I've discovered in most of my travels over the past decades.

Join me now for a trip outside the familiar world of microwaves, VCRs, and supermarkets into the uncomfortable world of cornu-*scarcity*.

It's axiomatic that the farther you and I are removed from a problem, the less concerned we tend to be. Go ahead, ask someone about Mozambique, and he or she won't have the foggiest notion where Mozambique is. Some may think it's an island in the Pacific. Others might place it who knows where. And yet, three million people are at risk in Mozambique. I'm sure you'd agree there is great room for improvement in our grasp of global needs.

World hunger is not improving. When the Club of Rome took an official look at international hunger in the early seventies, it felt there could be some possible improvement in the decade to follow. There's been little or no improvement.

World population will approach the six billion mark in the next decade. There will be more people dying of hunger in the next decade than in the past. No question about it. Even though you and I have enough food to feed the world, the gaps in the delivery system, coupled with human greed, keep us from making the big changes required.

However, whatever may be the reasons for today's status quo, I find any such defense totally unacceptable.

Every night one billion people in our world population of five billion go to bed hungry.

Seven hundred and eighty million live in *absolute* poverty (about 15 percent of the total world population). According to the World Bank, absolute poverty is a clearly defined category that represents a condition of life so characterized by malnutrition, illiteracy, and disease as to be beneath any reasonable definition of human decency.

Below even this level, 500 million totter at the edge of starvation. Consider the daily tally of 40,000 people, mostly children, who die of starvation. That's more than 1,600 per hour; fourteen and a half million every year.

Some people view such information with pessimism. But I have always been and will always be an optimist—as you will discover in later chapters. However, some of the contrasts involved in these issues push my optimism to its outer limits.

The six nations of the Sahel, that stretch of beleaguered desert which is home for the poorest and least developed of the earth, have experienced the worst drought in Africa's recorded history. It began in 1968. The 1975 harvest was much lower than had been anticipated, and experts working in the Sahel see no end to the cycle of drought, famine, and death.

There are thousands of children with matchstick legs, protruding ribs, and swollen stomachs, all the result of a relentless, prolonged malnutrition. Yacouba is one such child. He barely survives by eating boiled tree bark and roots. Those in his village pillage anthills to get at grain kernels insects have stored away. At least thirty million people like Yacouba live on the edge of ignominious, horrible death.

Wherever such tragedy stalks there is always the temptation to give up hope. Some victims have actually requested no medicines be provided them to combat typhus and cholera, since the absence of those medical miracles bring death more quickly (and hence more mercifully) than starvation.

Question: How does one begin to describe an African dirt farmer's agony as he watches his seeds lie idle in the parched earth for three years? How does one describe the panic and despair as precious water dries up? How does it feel to watch your last ox fall to the ground, or take apart your small house to sell the lumber for food?

Or how does one describe the feeling of parents unable to provide food for themselves or their children? What does a mother say to her children who are dying of malnutrition, crying for something to eat? And how do we grasp the horror that this brutal area of the Sahara desert is expanding at the rate of six to thirty miles per year?

From Ethiopia, we received reports of people so weakened from hunger that when a rainstorm hit the town, many drowned in two inches of water, unable to raise their heads from the gutter because of their utter weakness.

In the Danakil Desert, the nomadic tribesmen of Ethopia are in danger of dying out as a race. Carcasses of their cattle, sheep, goats, and camels litter the desert; the surviving animals are so scrawny they are being sold for less than five percent of their normal value. Some Danakil dead have been found with dirt in their stomachs, evidence that they have tried to lick the ground for moisture.

The frightening intensity of these human tragedies leaves me groping for language. I relate such facts not to make you feel guilty, but rather to help make you feel grateful and also aware of the world's need.

Most of us will never know what it is like to be really hungry.

Hunger hurts. It's debilitating. The starving body cannibalizes itself. It consumes its own fat, muscles, and tissues. Victims become listless, confused, unable to work or to think clearly. No one should have to *live* that way. More importantly, no one should have to *die* that way.

Hungry people are real people with real feelings, real hopes, real dreams. They are not mere images on TV screens or newspaper photos. If they seem small in our sight, that's because forty percent of them are children. Most of the remainder are women.

At the present rate, it is possible that four or five million people could starve in Ethiopia in the next eighteen months. An additional two million people are at risk in Mozambique. I wish I could say the situation was better in nations like Mali, Chad, and Sudan, but that would be wishful thinking.

That Makes Us Brothers

Let me tell you a story about a man and his five grand-children. I was in Chad in the southern Sudan, which is one of the two or three poorest countries in the world. As I walked through the World Vision camp it was hot and dusty. The wind was blowing and I found myself filled with anger. I was angry with World Vision because we weren't doing more. I was angry with myself . . . and with God. Then I saw this group of nine people who had just arrived at the camp. They caught my eye which is why I counted them and remembered it so well. "I want to go over and talk to this old gentleman," I told our World Vision workers.

The man in question had nothing more than a rag covering his body. I could see his rib cage as if it were a thin sheet of film stretched over a few sticks. With him were five little kids, naked, huddling under a small scrub brush where they had sought refuge from the sun's merciless rays. Through our interpreter I asked, "How long have you been traveling here from your country?" He didn't know if it was two weeks or three. He had no idea.

"Did you bring anything with you? Have you any food?" I asked.

"No, we haven't eaten until today."

He was grateful for the meager meal we were able to provide. We talked for a while. I pulled out a U.S. quarter and gave it to him.

"I want you to have this as a little momento of our visit."

He took it, looked at it, held it in the palm of his hand. But he didn't really pay it much attention.

So I asked him, "Do you have a coin from your country or from here that you can give to me as a remembrance of our conversation?"

He shook his head and said, no, he didn't have anything.

"Don't you have anything at all?" I asked further. "Did you bring your pots and pans with you?"

"No, we have nothing."

Then I said to this toothless old gentleman (I don't know how old he was. I'd guess he was seventy, perhaps, or eighty.) "I see you have some grandchildren. How many do you have?"

He held up his hand and counted, one, two, three, four, five, with his fingers.

"Well, I'm a grandfather too," I said, "and I have five grandchildren back in my country a long, long way away." And then I hugged the old man. I hugged him and said, "We're brothers. You have five grandchildren and I have five grandchildren. That makes us brothers."

At that point he responded for the first time. He smiled at me. As he did, I got choked up and went away a few yards and said to my Lord, "Why? Why should this happen to me? Here are my five grandchildren, well-parented, well-clothed, well-fed, well-schooled, and sometimes well-behaved. But why should I have those five and he has these five who may not survive another day?"

So I said to our World Vision team, "Please make sure this family is well taken care of. Train them in some skills. Also please make sure they hear and understand the gospel. Tell them we're feeding them and helping them because of the love of Christ." I went on, "The second oldest question asked in the Bible is in Genesis 4, 'Am I my brother's keeper?' Now I'm responsible for this man. I've talked to him and I'm responsible for his family and we'd better make sure they are taken care of."

To face a starving grandfather of five is far more compelling than reading a statistic or hearing an obscure report from some distant corner of our world. In many ways I wish you could accompany me on my travels to these lands and feel the urgency first hand. But at the same time I'm glad you don't. We need as many responsive "saviors" as possible. My job is to help make you feel like you've suffered alongside these victims while you're still back home, where it's possible to produce the dollars and goods we need to relieve the needs of these who suffer.

Five Factors

What has brought this widespread hunger to the world? Let me briefly outline five factors in the hunger equation that seem to be working together to produce this worldwide famine.

Famine Factor #1—Population Dynamics

Due to the effectiveness of modern medicine, the death rate for the world as a whole is still declining. In 1935, it was twenty-five deaths per 1000 persons; by 1980 it was twelve—just half the rate in less than half a decade.

Today nearly half of the people in underdeveloped countries are under the age of fifteen. In 1967, William and Paul Paddock wrote in their book, *Famine 1975,* "The people are already here who will cause the famines. Birth control techniques are for the future; they cannot affect the present millions of hungry stomachs."[1]

Another crucial element of the population dynamic is birth rate. This has skyrocketed in underdeveloped countries in recent years. Younger people are more fertile and are still reluctant to assume the obligation and risk to their future earning capacity imposed by family planning.

Until the eighteenth century, the world population growth rate was considerably below one percent per year. It has increased rapidly in the twentieth century, now doubling in thirty-five years. Five billion today. Six and a half billion by the year 2000. This is largely a result of the sharp rise in the population of all the Third World—or as they are often called, the two-thirds world countries.

For example, one out of six people on earth live and die in India. Each year this country alone produces 15,000,000 new mouths to feed. That's more than the entire population of Australia.

Thus we are seeing not only a significant, steady increase in the size of the population of the world, but a constant acceleration in the rate of growth. In spite of only moderate expansion in the industrialized countries, the population growth of the world as a whole is racing ahead at breakneck speed.

Famine Factor #2—Dwindling Food Supplies

In the last century, the English economist and clergyman, Thomas Malthus, taught the theory that periodic famines were inevitable because food production increases in an arithmetic progression (1, 2, 3, 4, 5, 6, etc.) while the population expands in a geometric progression (1, 2, 4, 8, 16, 32, etc.).

According to this theory, to feed these new mouths, the world must produce an additional thirty million tons of food each year—an increase of at least 2.5 percent—just to maintain present per capita consumption levels. For the developing countries, that's like walking on a treadmill—moving quickly, but going nowhere fast!

Yet as our population swells, cities creep deeper and deeper into the fertile countryside, replacing productive fields with factories, stores, and houses. Thus, less space is available to produce the huge amounts of grains needed to sustain an exploding population.

Consequently, the world's food reserves are at their lowest point in this century—barely enough to last for twenty-five days. *National Geographic* magazine described the situation graphically when it said that the international cupboard is almost bare.

Anothony J. Cernera, director of the educational programs for Bread for the World, talks about the seriousness of land reform. He believes that a continuing and fundamental problem in most developing countries is the tremendous inequality in the distribution of the rights to land. A significant proportion of the agricultural labor force is landless. For instance, he points out that in Latin America and the Caribbean, most of the arable land is held in large estates—and the proportion of people who are landless exceeds forty percent in such nations as Costa Rica, Argentina, Columbia, and Uruguay.

According to the World Bank, the landless in India is at thirty-two percent, while in Asia as a whole, thirty percent of the agricultural labor force is landless.

Agrarian reform is still the cry of millions from within the developing countries—reform that will lead first to equitable access to land, water, and other natural resources; second, to widespread sharing of economic and political power; third, to increasing and more productive employment; and fourth, to full participation and integration of rural people in the production and distribution systems of their respective countries.

Lappe and Collins in their book, *Food First*, point out that "... the world is producing each day two pounds of grain, or more than 3,000 calories, for every man, woman, and child on earth. . . . And this estimate is minimal. It does not include the many other staples such as beans, potatoes, cassava, rangefed meat, much less fruits and vegetables. The problem is not a shortage of food. The earth could provide an adequate diet for eight billion people, or nearly twice the present global population."[2]

This condition prompted my friend Senator Mark O. Hatfield to cite an appropriate verse from Proverbs during his remarks to government, business, and religious leaders in several African countries during a 1983 visit. "A poor man's field may produce abundant food, but injustice sweeps it away" (Prv 13:23, NIV).

Significant political and economic actions which transfer land to the people are an essential first step in the fight against hunger, poverty, and the problem of displaced people. And, although I remain an optimist, that seems to me to be a long way off.

Famine Factor #3—Affluence

In addition to the demands of an ever-expanding world population, affluence is emerging as a major new claimant on world food reserves. Rising expectations in Western Europe, Japan, Korea, Taiwan, and the Soviet Union—and, of course, the United States—have bred an insatiable desire in people to enjoy protein in the form of meat rather than vegetables.

Americans, for example, consume some 2,000 pounds of grain per capita per year, mostly in the form of meat, eggs, milk, and a variety of processed foods. In the developing nations, which tend to consume the grains directly rather than via animal products, average grain consumption is only about 400 pounds per year—one-fifth our consumption. The livestock of the rich world is in direct competition with the humans of the poor world.

Morrison's Cafeteria in Frankfort, Kentucky, serves about four hundred to five hundred people during an average lunch hour. According to the manager, the wasted food fills two thirty-gallon garbage containers daily.

It's a similar story at Les Champs Restaurant in New York. Mel Dansby says the eatery dumps at least ten pounds of butter and one hundred pounds of meat each week. That comes to two and one-half tons of meat and one quarter ton of butter each year, wasted, in one restaurant.

"I learned that 137 million tons of food—or more than twenty percent of this country's total annual food production—never find their way to the consumer and are either wasted or discarded," says Tony Hall, U.S. Congressman from Ohio who serves as chairman of the International Task Force of the Select Committee on Hunger.[3] As a result he organized a "Dumpster Luncheon" for Senators and Congressmen made up entirely of discarded or surplus food.

As for the future, some scholars predict food scarcity will become a normal condition of life on planet Earth—and not only in the poor nations, but in the richer ones as well. Will Americans, Europeans, and those of other growing, affluent, industrialized nations be willing to cut consumption to help the poor, starving people of the world? It all depends.

Richard J. Barnet writes in his book *The Lean Years: Politics in the Age of Scarcity,* "There are enough resources in the world to support a decent life for the predicted global population of the year 2000, but not to support lopsided opulence or continual ecological plunder."[4]

There are many who believe it doesn't have to be this way. Did God make a colossal mistake in his design of our world? Did he underestimate the need for food production? Or did the caretakers of the garden make some wrong choices? I'll have more to say on this subject in the pages that follow.

Famine Factor #4—Energy Consumption

Fuel shortages arising from the current worldwide energy crisis continue to have a powerful, direct influence on food production. Farmers, particularly those in overseas areas, find it difficult to locate fuel for their tractors and equipment. Further, there is a severe shortage of petroleum-based nitrogen fertilizers for those who till our land. These and other factors threaten to curb further "green revolution" improvement in the yield of such basic crops as corn, wheat, and rice.

Energy costs have tripled in recent years—affecting not only the production of foodstuffs but also distribution of those products. Producing a surplus in Kansas, Saskatchewan, or Queensland won't do much good for the starving in the Sudan if the cost of energy renders transportation impractical or impossible.

Famine Factor #5—Unfavorable Weather

Much of the world has experienced major drought in the past few years. The chances of enough decent food for millions of human beings may simply depend on the whims of one year's weather. Some climatologists believe the earth is undergoing the biggest shift in its climate in almost three hundred years. About ten years ago, scientists began noting that the high-altitude winds that ring the North Pole have shifted south, thus affecting weather patterns throughout the world.

The earth seems to be cooling off, and the process is causing a southward migration of the monsoon rains. This in turn is producing the dry-weather pattern stretching from the sub-Saharan drought belt through the Middle East to India, South Asia, and North China.

Rainfall from Mauritania in West Africa to India in 1970 was barely half what it was in 1957. Scientists are still baffled by the phenomenon. Some suspect it may have been caused by sunspots or increased carbon dioxide and dust in the air, or a combination of both.

In the spring of 1988 the Mississippi River valley in the United States experienced its worst drought in half a century. The mighty Mississippi fell so low that normal river traffic was choked to a standstill for a week until dredging operations could deepen the channel. Other rivers of the Midwest waterway also underwent extreme conditions. The Red River of the North in Grand Forks, North Dakota was down by seventy percent. The Saline River in Arkansas was off by ninety percent. The economic implications of such shortfalls are staggering.

By anyone's calculations, these five factors—population dynamics, dwindling food supplies, affluence, energy consumption, and unfavorable weather—add up to a formula for catastrophe.

Famine Factor #6—Political Unrest

The previous factors seem comprehensible as forces behind world famine. I can understand poor weather, low food production, energy problems, and the like in taking their toll on food production. But what I can't understand is the deliberate use of famine as a tool for political control. Sadly, I'm compelled to add yet another factor to our list of famine forces: that of politics.

Consider Ethiopia and the example we cited in chapter 1. Drought sears northern Ethiopia. It suffers through what relief workers call a "controlled famine." And what happens politically? Rebels attack a city and capture its field workers. The Marxist government then responds with further destruction or forced relocation of the populace. As we stated earlier, the resulting unrest has cut off nearly all supplies to distribution centers providing food for some 550,000 people. And the condition is not new. The saber of famine has disemboweled Ethiopia during nearly thirty years of civil war.

We see the same pattern in other troubled lands. Leftist forces in Nicaragua choke off food supplies and food production to stay in power. Dictators in Haiti line their cupboards at the expense of working people across the land. Even with a democratic power in control, this island nation is left with no reserves to build on. Hunger and hardship are the inevitable result.

Afghanistan struggles to throw off oppression, and the ruling power retaliates against farm implements, fruit trees, and livestock. Slogans and "isms" may differ, but similar hardships devour food production in the Sudan, Mali, Ghana, and numerous other countries.

Oppression to the point of blood is not required to leach the life out of a country. Political unrest in the form of economic confusion can also produce anemia. Brazil is so distorted by the weight of crushing national debt that it has resorted to slash and burn tactics against the fragile Amazonian rain forests to seize quick profits. The result is short term gain for selected food producers and the federal coffers, but long term disaster for the nation as a whole. These same tactics transformed northern Africa from the breadbasket of the world during the time of ancient Rome into the Sahara desert of today. Costa Rica, the quiet country whose President earned a Nobel peace prize for his role in Central American mediation, is waging the same economic war against its own irreplaceable rain forests.

Be it economic or military unrest, political pressure for quick results often butchers the ox that plows the field.

Our Worlds Are Numbered

Who are these people of the "Second" and "Third Worlds?"

Time magazine is credited with popularizing this numbering system. The "First World" is the free societies of the West. The "Second" is the communist bloc nations, "Third" is the developing nations, and the "Fourth" is the underdeveloped nations.

I'm not entirely comfortable with these labels. To speak of the "Third" or "Fourth World" has elements of resentment built in. These seem to imply that the goal for all should be to be like the "First World"—the Western free nations. If authorities kept referring to earth as "the third planet," how long would it be before we became obsessed with a desire to migrate to the "first planet?"

The label Third World often represents the same sort of condescending attitude one would use toward an adolescent. It can imply that the people within a country are only at the fledgling stages of national "puberty," with *true* nationhood coming only when they adopt the ways of a more mature, adult, and civilized culture (such as the West).

And a more philosophical question. How can there be more than one world on the same planet? The animal world has no chance of joining the plant world (apart from a few biological oddities such as sponges or rare "animal plants"). The mineral world is distinct from the world of music, from the world of finance, from the world of language. We conveniently place concepts in a separate world because it's the only way we can make them fit. This troubles me when I think about the "Third World." Do its people have no right to exist in the Second or First World?

An alternate approach toward understanding the so-called *Third World* is to think of the world in a geographical context. Draw a line around the globe through northern Mexico, across the northern tip of Africa, continue it over the top of the Middle East, India, and China. Now, above that line, the northern "half of the world," as it were, will have countries with a quality of life that far exceeds the southern "half" in life expectancy, infant mortality, literacy, and general economic well-being.

With few exceptions (notably Australia, New Zealand, and South Africa), the southern "half" of the globe comprises the developing world. The external conflicts between the developed and the developing world can also be viewed as a North-South conflict. Many are using this terminology in their writing today.

We in the West, or North, may tend to be overly defensive, or perhaps even guilt-ridden, when trying to discern the actual facts regarding the problems and tensions between North and South. In most cases, the root of the turmoil seems to be over the development of a new economic order. Increasingly, the South or Third World is making demands for such a new order, and the North is not quite sure what it will mean—or what it will all lead to. Justice and liberation are terms often used, terms that often strike terror in the hearts of the affluent North.

Since the North is often viewed as the "arch-aggressor of modern times," according to Arnold Toynbee, we are perhaps naturally defensive. Be that as it may, there is a tremendous need for greater sensitivity, understanding, and a capacity to empathize with the concerns of our brothers and sisters in the South.

Mature, developing countries are not asking for handouts. Rather, they want and deserve encouragement, respect, and access to a fair share of their piece of this economic pie. Having said that, I remain a firm believer in the free enterprise system, and in spite of its failures, cannot imagine a better system than the democratic way of life and the promise it holds for all.

I agree with Anthony Cernera of Bread for the World who believes that the primary task of those in the U.S. concerned about international social justice should be one of education. We need to enlarge the community of those who see the interrelationship between rural development, international trade, and world survival. People living in developed nations must realize the interdependent nature of our world.

When we attain a more enlightened understanding of the interrelationship between peoples and a deeper trust between the developed nations and the countries of Africa, Asia, and Latin America, then we can develop long-range public policy that will achieve a more just economic order.

The needs of the world are much deeper than political freedom and security, deeper than social and economic development, deeper than democracy and progress. The need of the world belongs to a sphere of the mind, the heart, and the spirit, a sphere to be penetrated with the light and grace of Jesus Christ.

What must we do to penetrate this sphere of the mind? I share the conviction of the late Dr. Malik in looking for the light and grace of our Savior. But where does this leave you and me? Simply knowing the factors is not enough. Understanding how to count the different worlds will never offset the massive number of missing food shipments. With our knowledge must come action, or we simply play a cruel, deadly game.

Robert McAfee Brown writes in "Other Eyes, Other Voices,"

> Quite frankly, many born-again Latin American believers don't even believe we are Christians. They ask, how could we possibly be Christians when we live lifestyles of such evident greed and self-interest while Christians in other parts of the world don't have enough to eat? They ask how can we be Christians when we support economic and political systems that are crushing them?[5]

Too often these problems seem remote. The lands are distant, customs strange to us, names hard to pronounce. But how would you react if the severest form of hunger and poverty were in your backyard?

Have you looked across your back fence at night? Are you entirely sure there isn't a hungry, homeless person (or family) living in the shrubs under the cover of the night?

Our next chapter sheds some harsh light on one of the darker secrets in our "developed" country, the poor and hungry among us.

You don't have to go halfway across the world to witness misplaced priorities. Go back to your hometown and watch them trade in the tools of agricultural productivity for the trinkets of materialistic ease.

THREE

Across Town, Across the Street, a Cross to Bear

I**T'S AN UNBELIEVABLE PICTURE.** A young man stands with a dazed look on his face, his hair and eyebrows frozen in snow, the front of his jacket and sweater totally white. But he doesn't live in the Yukon or Siberia. His picture was taken on the streets of New York in February and published in the book *Homeless in America: A Photographic Project.*[1]

The remarks of his photographer are equally shocking. "He was completely encrusted in snow, and when I looked down at his feet I realized with some horror that he wasn't wearing socks." Nancy Elliott offered him a hot cup of coffee. He politely declined, kicked the snow from his instep and went on his way with "an unmistakable air of dignity."[2]

This ice man is but one of an estimated 350,000 homeless victims in America. Some place the number as high as three million (over the course of a year). And unlike the derelicts and the so-called skid row bums of past years, the fastest growing categories among the homeless are women, children, and young families.

It's easy to dismiss the problem of hunger, pain, and poverty when the victims live half a world away. It's another story when the starving souls live only half a block away.

In a *Newsweek* article on the homeless, Tom Mathews writes, "A recent national poll ranked homelessness as America's number two problem—directly behind the deficit (and well ahead of the nuclear arms race and AIDS). Better than eight out of ten Americans now say the issue embarrasses them."[3]

It will take more than embarrassment to rid ourselves of this problem. According to one activist's guess in this same issue of *Newsweek*, the bill for housing the homeless could run as high as $20 billion a year for fifteen years. That's over $300 billion by the first of the new century.

Homelessness isn't the only ticket to deprivation. Even those with adequate housing can find themselves squeezed in the grip of poverty. America's "hidden poor" account for the largest share of victims. With the official definition of poverty set at $11,203 annual cash income for a family of four, most people assume the greatest number live in the crowded inner city and subsist on welfare.

Not so. One recent report cited by *U.S. News and World Report* from Harvard's Center for Health and Human Resources Policy found that "even if every poor resident of the poorest neighborhoods in the nation's 100 largest cities in 1980 were counted as a member of the underclass, that hard-core group would amount to only seven percent of the nation's poor."[4]

Surprisingly, the majority of poor in America have jobs.

Unlike the welfare poor, whose numbers have risen only modestly in the last decade, the number of working poor has mushroomed. There are now nine million poor adults who work, and the problem is particularly acute for those of prime working age. From 1978 to 1986, the number of poor adults age 22 to 64 who averaged thirty weeks or more of work a year rose 52 percent—and now includes almost seven million Americans. An unexpected number of working poor toil long hours at low wages. In 1986, two million Americans worked full-time throughout the entire year and were still poor—an increase of more than fifty percent since 1978.[5]

This is taking place in the United States—the country long looked upon as the economic savior of the world. But if America cannot support her own, what of the waiting millions across the sea?

Because I live in America and because this country is universally looked upon as a role model, this chapter focuses primarily on the United States. But the fundamental lessons learned from disadvantaged people in Chicago, Miami, Los Angeles, or Seattle are applicable to Montreal, London, Paris, Rio de Janeiro, Tokyo, or Johannesburg.

In our last chapter we discovered a man-made division between the developed nations of the North and the developing nations of the South. But upon closer examination, we also discover a bifurcation in the world between people on opposite sides of the same boulevard.

Homeless derelicts camp out on the steam vents in Washington, D.C. directly across the street from government offices. A family of eleven struggles to eke out a living on $7,600 in annual earnings across town from a childless couple spending easily that much on ski trips and cruises.

The way we treat a needy person on the street of our own town reveals a great deal about the way we look at the needy half a world away. How can you and I expect to make lasting progress toward reducing world hunger if we are unwilling to take up the difficult cross of civic hunger in our own communities?

Where They Come From

Perhaps it's just too easy to feel smug about the disadvantaged. Judgments of "How could someone allow themselves to come to that?" rise to the fore.

Beware. Jonathan Kozol, author of a best-selling work on

the subject of America's poor, writes, "A lot of good working people in the United States are just three paychecks and one bad operation, one cancer diagnosis, one emergency away from homelessness."[6]

In researching his book, *Rachel and Her Children: Homeless Families in America,* Kozol learned fate can be cruel.

While working on *Rachel and Her Children,* he met an acquaintance he had known as a teaching assistant at the University of Wisconsin. A former high school teacher, the man had gotten sick, lost his job, and his wife had been hospitalized for depression. His money gone, the man had become homeless and was living in the Martinique (hotel for transients) when Kozol began researching his book.

"When I see that, I figure it could happen to you or me," he says.[7]

Alice in Terrorland

Alice is a middle aged woman who has been getting her daily sustenance from trash bins for most of this decade. She recounted her story to a college student while foraging in a dumpster outside a fast food restaurant in Los Angeles.

She told me she had led a pretty normal life as she grew up and eventually went to college. From there she went on to Chicago to teach school. She was single and lived in a small apartment.

One night, after she got off the train after school, a man began to follow her to her apartment building. When she got to her door she saw a knife and the man hovering behind her. She had no choice but to let him in. The man raped her.

After that, things got steadily worse. She had a nervous breakdown. She went to a mental institution for three months, and when she went back to her apartment she found her belongings gone. The landlord had sold them to cover the rent she hadn't paid.

She had no place to go and no job because the school had terminated her employment. She slipped into depression. She lived with friends until she could muster enough money for a ticket to Los Angeles. She said she no longer wanted to burden her friends, and that if she had to live outside, at least Los Angeles was warmer than Chicago.

It is as if she began back then to take on the mentality of a street person. She resolved herself to homelessness. She's been out west since 1980, without a home or job. She seems happy, with her best friend being her cat. But the scars of memories still haunt her, and she is running from them, or should I say "him."[8]

I'm not trying to put you on the defensive, but I must ask you and me these questions: What feelings do you and I have when we dress up for a downtown occasion and walk past a dirty man staring glassy-eyed in the alley? How do you and I feel about coming out of a gleaming bank lobby with several crisp twenty dollar bills in our wallets or purses when we encounter a disheveled woman pawing through the trash?

I appreciate these words and deeds from a woman of action, Constance Parvey, as recounted in a recent issue of *Christianity and Crisis.*

In 1983, when I came back to the U.S. after working in Switzerland with the World Council of Churches, I saw women eating out of the trash bins in the now fashionable Faneuil Hall section of Boston, and in Cambridge there were "Shopping Bag Ladies" in Harvard Square, mostly white and mostly elderly. At night in Coply Square, women and children were sleeping in the doorways of Back Bay churches. I had trouble "adjusting" to what I was seeing. What I had witnessed on the streets of Calcutta and Jakarta, I did not expect to find in Boston.

Now in 1987, living in Philadelphia, I continue to see women living on the grates. Finally, last year I decided to cross the barrier and meet some of them. Through a friend who works with the Philadelphia Committee for the Homeless, I started volunteering to work on the streets. The volunteers meet at the Broad Street center. We are assigned in groups of three to cover different geographical areas of the inner city where the majority of the homeless street people live. Dressed in layers of clothes, with extra scarves, mittens, and blankets, we start out on Friday nights for the two-hour rounds. One person carries a gallon thermos of hot tea, another an insulated picnic basket with warm casseroles, and a third has the sandwiches, styrofoam cups, and granola bars. We look like we are headed for a winter picnic, or are homeless people ourselves. Our rounds go from grate to grate, As we approach, we greet people, kneel down to their level, introduce ourselves by first names, and if they don't reciprocate, we ask for theirs.

We don't assume they want anything. We ask them if they want something to eat, if they need anything, if they would rather be in a shelter, In general we express our concern and try to find out how they are faring. Most of the people are appreciative, compliant, passive, and happy to see us. They say "Thank you," and some say "God bless you." A few let us know that they don't like "do-gooders" and "hand-outs," and occasionally one is too shy, frightened, proud, or confused to say anything, or to ask for anything.[9]

Looking Upward

Many poor and homeless people are doing everthing within their power to advance. But they still need help from those in the ranks above. What they don't need is people looking down on them with revulsion or pity.

Ramona Parish dropped out of school and married at the age of sixteen. The next chapter of her life is woefully predictable. Now with three children and no husband she lives on Aid to Families with Dependent Children (AFDC) and is trying to piece together a future as a legal secretary.

Ramona would be easy to look down upon as nothing more than another "welfare" woman. But she took the initiative to write a personal article for *Newsweek* entitled, "Messages From a Welfare Mom." It says a great deal about what people in her condition need in order to prevail.

I cannot survive on $3.35 per hour with three children, without regular child-support payments or health insurance. So I live on AFDC and often feel guilty because I take advantage of this system and its services. But I'm also made to feel ashamed because I cannot pay for things with my own hard-earned money.

To my ex-husband: Why should I have been the one who was embarrassed when your father stopped by and gave our son a pair of tennis shoes and each of our two daughters $10? You should be the one who is embarrassed.

To all doctors and dentists: Would my hysterectomy which was done three years ago when I was only twenty-eight have been so urgent if I hadn't had Medicaid to pay for it? Could I have avoided taking estrogen every day for the rest of my life?

... After several extractions—six teeth lost in the six years on AFDC with three more to go soon—I find it difficult to chew my food properly. It's a standard joke now that I'm always the last one to leave the table; in reality, I'm too embarrassed to tell people that dentists suggest pulling teeth because Medicaid won't pay for root canals and crowns.

To all social-service workers: When I am willing to help myself and work, why do you take everything away? Can't you at least let me keep the food stamps and medical insurance until I'm above the poverty level? Without these benefits I cannot make it, so I stay on the soaring welfare rolls. I don't want a free ride, but I do need a lift.[10]

Breadloser

Another telling story about the long climb upward is the case of a homeless man in sportscoat and tie. Only months ago Jerry Neuman was a typical family man and middle-class breadwinner. "With me, it happened to be a bout with thyroid cancer and not being able to work for a period of time and getting divorced in the interim" that wiped out his savings and left him destitute, Jerry said.

But despite his new address—Greyhound bus terminal or beneath a highway overpass—Jerry struggles to stay neat and well groomed. He is moved with passion about a plan to build group homes for those homeless who are willing and able to work and want to get back into society.

That desire brought him to Los Angeles City Hall one day for a surprising encounter. Dressed in better-than-he-can-afford clothes, Jerry came to city hall to hear homeless activist Ted Hayes lobby for improvement. Hayes declared that rich people are dying to give their money away for the cause. "I'll bet you could write me a check right now for $1,000," Hayes said to our man in his blue suit and trench coat.

"Are you sure?" came the reply.

"Well if not $1,000, I know you can write a check for $500," said the advocate.

"As a matter of fact," said Jerry Neuman, "I sleep on the streets of this city every night. I am homeless."[11]

As with most issues, things are not always as they appear. Jerry Neuman struggles to keep up the appearances of normalcy to help himself and other homeless victims regain a place in line for the cornucopia. He feels he understands their needs on a more personal basis.

"Little things, like telephone calls, become insurmountable," he said. You and I can make a local phone call for a few pennies, as part of the monthly rate.

"I make a phone call from a Greyhound bus terminal to someone who lives in Beverly Hills and it costs me fifty cents for the first three minutes and a nickel a minute after that," Neuman relates.

Then there is the job interview to contend with.

"A homeless person cannot (afford to) buy a monthly bus pass with unlimited transportation.... He drops eighty-five or ninety cents or a buck fifty if it's out of the third zone each and every time he gets on that bus. You can spend ten dollars and accomplish nothing," Neuman said.

"And then it gets down to a matter of am I going to spend ten dollars to talk to this person or am I going to go get something to eat and make damn sure I'm clean and make sure I've got enough money to sit in the bus terminal and drink coffee all night."

Here is a man who is highly motivated and well-possessed of his faculties. What does he think of the realities of spending the night outdoors and unprotected?

About his first night on the streets, "The one thing I remember feeling is the fear of it getting dark at night. That's a very, very, very frightening feeling. Late in the afternoon you get this anxiety [about finding a place to sleep] and you still get it even after a couple of months."

Again I point out, Jerry Neuman is a well-dressed, normal thinking person. What of the sick and incompetent who make up such a large portion of the homeless?

Roll Call of the Homeless

Look at the various categories which make up the single term we call "homeless." How prepared are they to take care of themselves and satisfy this hunger for belonging?

Veterans, mainly from the Vietnam War. In many American cities, vets make up close to fifty percent of all homeless males.

The mentally ill. In some parts of the country, roughly a quarter of the homeless would have been institutionalized a couple of decades ago.

The physically disabled or chronically ill, who do not receive any benefits or whose benefits do not enable them to afford permanent shelter.

The elderly on fixed incomes whose funds are no longer sufficient for their needs.

Men, women, and whole families pauperized by the loss of a job.

Single parents, usually women, without the resources or skills to establish new lives.

Runaway children, many of whom have been abused.

Alcoholics and those in trouble with drugs (whose troubles often begin with one of the other conditions listed here).

Immigrants, both legal and illegal, who often are not counted among the homeless because they constitute a separate "problem."

Traditional tramps, hobos, and transients, who have taken to the road or the streets for a variety of reasons and who prefer to be there.[12]

Is this army of casualties strewn across the battlefield of daily existence because we do not have enough money for ammunition? If these stories were coming from Nicaragua, Cambodia, or Uganda I might agree. But this is America, one of the richest, most well-fed countries in recorded history. What shortage here leaves these victims cold and hungry?

A passage from 1 John comes to mind as a blistering indictment.

> But whoever has the world's goods, and beholds his brother in need and closes his heart against him, how does the love of God abide in him? (1 Jn 3:17, NASB)

I'll have more to say about the power of God's love to feed the hungry in chapters to come.

Suburban Wasteland

Wasted people are not the only cause of poverty. Chapter 1 discussed the problems of land abuse. It's not difficult to picture a heartless corporation robbing peasants of their rightful property in some faraway tropical country. It's not difficult to correlate communist farming policies with food shortage. We can understand the damage caused by drought, flood, fire, or other natural disaster. But what is difficult to comprehend is how responsible leaders can permit (and often encourage) fertile land to drop out of production.

I was struck by this first-hand reaction from Tom Sine to the advance of shopping centers, parking lots, and suburban sprawl in his hometown.

> I remember the sick feeling in the pit of my stomach as I watched bulldozers scrape down square miles of apricot orchards still laden with fruit in San Jose during the sixties. In less than a decade, San Jose was transformed from the fruit and nut center of California to a suburban wasteland. As we approach the year 2000, the regions in California and Florida on which we have become dependent for our winter fruit and vegetables are slowly succumbing to the developers. Florida is projected to develop almost all of its prime farmland by the year 2000.[13]

Just as "third-world-like" people inhabit the alleys and gutters of America, so do "third-world-like" land priorities. As a society—and it's not only the U.S.—have we become so enthralled with the trappings of success (shopping centers, tract homes, super highways, etc.) that we forget where these luxuries came from in the first place (fields, orchards, pastures, forests, and waterways)? You don't have to go halfway across the world to witness misplaced priorities. Go back to your hometown and watch them trade in the tools of agricultural productivity for the trinkets of materialistic ease.

What Is Needed?

Certainly, there have been bright spots in the battle against domestic hunger. The "Live Aid" concerts of several years ago did much to make people aware of issues. "Hands Across America" gave thousands of citizens first-hand involvement with the needs. World Vision television specials likewise alerted hundreds of thousands to the need.

Gleaning projects offer tangible hope. Gleaning is a practice that originated in biblical times. It refers to gathering leftover crops in a field after the harvest and giving them to the poor or needy. In a year's time in this country, about sixty million tons of grain, fruit, and vegetables worth about five billion dollars are left in the fields to rot. Through gleaning projects, local non-profit organizations, volunteer, and church groups send people into the fields of participating farmers to collect the leftover food for distribution to the needy. One organization in Ohio gleaned almost 15,000 pounds of food and contributed to over 10,000 meals for needy people.

Other innovative programs gather surplus restaurant food or collect canned goods as part of the admission fee at large sporting events.

Much *is* being done.

But more is needed—from *you* and from *me*. It is staggering to contemplate that about twenty million Americans go hungry for part of each month. Some 35.5 million Americans live below the poverty line, and doctors have found "third-world-like" malnutrition among children in major American cities.[14]

The tragic outcome of poverty in America is not limited to the hardship and deprivation suffered by individual victims. Though depressed and malnourished, most of these victims are not in mortal danger. The real tragedy is the lost opportunity these people represent toward helping the chronically poor overseas. America, Western Europe, Japan, Canada, and other "haves" possess the resources and know-how to build spacecraft, mine the oceans, and perform the miracles required to help eradicate world hunger. But every bag lady in London, every poor working family in Bonn, every single parent on AFDC in Chicago, every derelict in the gutter of Tokyo or

Taipei erodes our ability to mobilize this vast potential.

I'm not saying we should ignore our own needy men, women, and children. I'm saying we should elevate the standard of every citizen in our world to the point where thousands more can take an active interest in the mission of reducing world hunger.

Much of the international community has looked to America for the past forty years for deliverance. Now, who will deliver the deliverer?

I don't know. Perhaps we in the West will have to go through some brutal shaking to wake us up to the seriousness of these problems at home and around the world. Most of us have never really known hunger as a lasting national experience. Yes, there are the homeless and poverty-stricken today. But that's only a small segment of our society—too easily pushed into the shadows. And yes, we went through the great depression. But that was only temporary. It failed to dull our persistent perception that America deserves to be rich and overfed.

I look at what happened to Christians in China. There, our brothers and sisters suffered brutally for their beliefs. During the revivals of 1949 and 1950 there were roughly three million Christians willing to stand up to the bullets and blades of a godless communism. Today it's estimated there are some fifty million believers in China. It's true: "The blood of the martyr *is* the seed of the church." Is that what it's going to take to broadcast the seeds of care and concern for today's starving masses? If we won't feel empathy and concern when the problem is thousands of miles across the sea, must we then learn such compassion by experiencing the same hunger at our own front door on a massive scale?

Hopefully not. The starving peoples of our world just don't have that much time.

So as you and I take up our cross of poverty and hunger in America, Europe, and throughout our world, it's my prayer we do not linger at the "poison pantry," our topic in chapter 4.

A climb toward unbridled materialism has cloyed the taste of millions. The search for an upwardly mobile lifestyle keeps leading us away from the upwardly permanent values of God and Christ.

FOUR

Poison Pantry

M ANY CONSUMERS ARE ENTHRALLED TODAY by the new genre of foods marketed as "light," "low fat," "sugar free," or "natural." These products seemingly promise indulgence without guilt; enjoyment without acceptable compromise. But they may not be the free meal ticket we have hoped for. For example, according to a nutrition column in my local newspaper, one brand of oats is advertised as particularly healthful because of its bran content, when in fact it may be one of the more harmful cereals you could possibly eat. After all, it's made with coconut oil, which has twice the saturated fat content of lard. And it's common knowledge that saturated fats raise the level of cholesterol.

Saccharin was once thought to be the cure-all replacement for sugar. Supposedly it could pack our sweet tooth without packing our waistlines. Now saccharin has been linked to cancer in animals and comes with a warning on the package limiting its use to those who must restrict sugar in their diet.

My point is this: Those products which invite us to overindulge don't tell the whole story. The miracle food in the pantry may well be a poison in disguise. This is not one layman's tirade against edible innovation. Rather, it's a call to reality. Those things which appear too good to be true usually are. It's that way in nutrition. It's also that way in ideas.

Artificial Chaff

This chapter is a survey of ideas which purport to be "whole wheat" and "natural" but are in reality artificial chaff. How can we digest any lasting thoughts on hunger if we're bloated with vacuous ideas?

Numerous "tares" choke out the grains of progress in our fight against hunger. Some sprout up in the physical realm, others the spiritual.

Physical obstacles include natural forces (such as drought, monsoon, hurricanes), transportation, distribution, finances, etc.

Spiritual obstacles, though less visible, are every bit as destructive to our efforts to relieve hunger. These include apathy, greed, jealousy, vanity, and "spiritual hosts of wickedness in heavenly places" (Eph 6:12).

And if having such tares in the field weren't enough, now these have been harvested, milled, refined, prepared, and delivered to our own private pantries. Too many spiritual larders are overstocked with counterfeit cures and empty calories. Escapism, hedonism, materialism, paganism, and a seductive "New Age" religion serve as a less than nourishing fast food for the soul. They may be satisfying to the tongue and filling to the stomach, but they damage the system. As you'll discover in this chapter, you don't have to go into the field to glean some heresy; most of it is within easy reach.

One Man's Meat . . .

Let's examine some of the stagnant ideas masquerading as staple food for Christian thought.

Physiologists tell us the tongue is able to discern only four basic tastes. From these—sweet, sour, salty, and bitter—come all the rich variety of flavors we enjoy. (I never could understand why they didn't include "hot" in this list. Maybe it's because you taste hot with more than your tongue. I must have hot buds on my lips, throat, forehead, and eyeballs.)

These four taste sensations (which allow us to enjoy our food) sometimes lure us to overeat or mis-eat. Therefore sweet, sour, salty, and bitter serve as a fitting outline for our review of orders and disorders of the spiritual appetite.

The Sweet Life

From our earliest days on mother's milk and baby formula, we develop a taste for sweetness. And because our taste buds are most receptive when we're young, many people develop a sweet tooth before they even grow any teeth. We expect things to be sweet.

This is acceptable with immature youngsters. But many people spill this same expectation onto their perceptions of life as a whole. They want the easy, comfortable, sweet life. And if that's not available, they reach for a pacifier.

Here in the United States, we call this the "American Dream." Beyond food, shelter, and clothing, we tend to expect society to deliver us a prestigious job, home ownership, personal transportation, and endless entertainment. After all, wasn't this nation founded on "the unalienable rights of life, liberty, and the *pursuit of happiness?*"

A climb toward unbridled materialism has cloyed the taste of millions. The search for an upwardly mobile lifestyle keeps leading us away from the upwardly permanent values of God, Christ, and the Bible.

Even those of us in the Christian community are enticed by a brand of Christian hedonism. It's easy to fall into the trap of thinking, "God exists to make me happy." Tom Sine warns:

We need to ask ourselves whether we are educating our young in the values of Jesus or in the values of the dominant national culture. Does the "hidden curriculum" of American culture, which emphasizes the values of materialism, individualism, and nationalism, have the upper hand, or do the "other-serving" values of Jesus have the greatest influence in our Christian educational systems? In all honesty, are our church schools, day schools, Christian colleges, and seminaries educating the young to fit into society or change it?[1]

Just as the Proverbs remind us "it is not good to eat much honey" (Prv 25:16, 27), so we need to evaluate the effects of overindulgence in the sweet life of ease.

Going Sour

The taste for sour food requires a great deal of faith. I'm reminded of that every time I see someone pour sour milk into a batch of biscuits or pancakes. Things sour when they spoil and our instincts tend to recoil at the sight. Only an accomplished cook can transform sour to superb.

But what happens when our faith goes sour? In the past, teachers were free to call upon biblical precepts to explain their own moral authority. Now, says Ruby Sitea, a teacher of values at Pacific High School in Brooklyn, New York as quoted in *Newsweek*, "we're talking about the conversion of what was moral under religion into what is moral for society."[2]

This curdling process reduces the available menu of values. When the Baltimore County, Maryland, school district first set about adopting a "common core of values" in the early 80s, it convened a round table on how best to instill compassion, courtesy, honesty, and tolerance in young students. Recalls associate superintendent Mary Ellen Saterlie, "A fundamentalist minister asked one of the best questions: 'Who or what is your moral example?' He said he could use the Bible and Jesus Christ. We obviously could not. We finally concluded that the Constitution and the Bill of Rights would be our moral example."[3]

Many students today have gone sour with a sense of impotence and fatalism on the large issues. About the future of America or the future of the world, they say, "It's going down the tubes and there's nothing we can do about it." With an attitude like that, students think they might as well enjoy themselves. In his book, *When Dreams and Heroes Died,* Arthur Levine labels this hedonism "going first class on the Titanic."

A Twenty-Year Study, 1966-85 observed that in 1967, 83 percent of entering freshmen believed it was "essential or very important to develop a meaningful philosophy of life," whereas in 1985 only 43 percent affirmed that proposition.[4]

Such a souring of spiritual provender leads to the search for new forms of nourishment. Most established religions aren't growing any faster than the rate of population increase. Since 1900 the population has tripled. Predictably, so has the number of Hindus, Roman Catholics, and Protestants. Even Islam has increased fourfold. In contrast, *Moody* magazine tells us, cultic religious movements (less than 200 years old) "have increased in membership this century by a factor of eighteen. More than 108 million people worldwide now belong to such groups."[5]

Numbered among these cults and new religions are such organizations as the Mormons, Jehovah's Witnesses, Church of Scientology, Christian Science, Unification Church, Hare Krishna, plus other splinters and offshoots.

Also fermenting is the New Age movement with its old age occultism. This spiritual whey is not a sect or cult. Instead, it contains a potpourri of organizations and individuals. These interpret the Eastern religious concepts of pantheism (all is god, therefore you are god) and reincarnation in terms of

Western humanistic science, philosophy, and psychology including self-realization and universal love. Hundreds of thousands of activists are working to transform society and bring about the "New Age." Shirley MacLaine is probably the most well-known advocate, with two books and a television miniseries on the subject.

Some thirty million Americans believe in one of the main tenets of this philosophy, reincarnation. Roughly seventy million claim to have experienced extrasensory perception.[6]

"Most of us who call ourselves Christians . . . live like pagans, think like pagans, and use the pagan view of the world." So begin the early paragraphs of an article entitled "Becoming Pagan," by Mike Yaconelli as published in the *Wittenburg Door.*[7]

What are the elements of paganism which have infiltrated our thinking, our lifestyles, our everyday existence, and have become so familiar that, according to Mike Yaconelli, "we can't identify them any longer?"

Here are five strains of modern paganism which the author of this article feels "have slowly contaminated our Christian faith."

1. The Legitimization of Self-Interest. Do we still believe that Jesus is first, others are second, and ourselves, last? For many Jesus is first as long as Jesus benefits ME. We are willing to put the self last "if putting myself last guarantees that I will be first." Many people are incapable of understanding that Christianity costs them anything.

2. The Belief that Pain and Suffering Are Not to Be Expected. People used to accept the idea that pain and suffering brought meaningful lessons. "We no longer believe that. And it goes much deeper than 'pain and suffering.' Modern Christians believe that *any* discomfort, *any* struggle, *any* period of doubt or waiting need not be." Yaconelli feels we have given new meaning to the term "soft." According to him we are more than soft, we are incapable of perseverance, of patience, and of long-suffering.

3. The Belief that There Are No Moral Absolutes. John Naisbitt has spoken of a "multiple option" society free of any absolutes. Personal choice reigns as the only moral reference. "The ramifications of this new moral openness are deep and frightening," observes Yaconelli in his explanation of these principles on modern paganism. "More and more people in our society do not believe in evil."

4. The Erosion of Personal Responsibility. People used to believe they were responsible for their actions. That assumption has faded. Is your child not doing well in school? Whose fault is it? Certainly not yours. It must be because of the teacher, the school district, the principal—anyone but you. Is it your fault if you slip and fall on the sidewalk? "No way," mimics Yaconelli. It is the city's fault, the cement maker's fault, or the fault of the designer. Why wasn't a sign put up warning people they could fall?

5. The Denial of Consequence. How many people believe what they do affects someone else? "If what I do appears to affect someone else, then they have a problem—not me . . . we are bewildered when other people's lives are disrupted by our behavior." Ask yourself. Has our thinking been so altered by this culture that we actually believe God will protect us from experiencing any consequences of our behavior? Mike Yaconelli reprinted a letter from a church youth group. There the members were graciously soliciting money on behalf of a girl who took her parents' car without permission and caused $2,300 worth of damage. Too often we assume the consequences of our actions belong to others.

This process of becoming sour on God and turning to other deities reminds me of a graphic proverb. (If you're eating something right now you may want to finish your bite before reading on.) There are few things in life as sour and disgusting as partially digested food. The Apostle Peter confronted the people of his day who wanted to turn from the "bread of life" to other more attractive sustenance with this observation: "But it has happened to them according to the true proverb: 'A dog returns to his own vomit'" (2 Pt 2:22).

I contend we cannot solve the problems of international hunger unless we keep fresh before us the truth of God.

Salt Rations

In discussing the sensation of sweetness I suggested it was the earliest taste we recall, harking back to our need for mother's milk. But is it possible we encountered an even earlier taste? In the past few decades, the wonders of technology have revealed the greater wonders of God's creation. I'm referring to those hypnotic pictures most of us have seen from the surreal world of the unborn. As no society in all of recorded history, we can observe the tiny preborn in a sea of salt water laughing, crying, and suckling. There King David's royal observation becomes even more majestic, "I am fearfully and wonderfully made" (Ps 139:14).

Could there be any more primal taste sensation than that which we experienced the split second our taste buds were linked to our brain? And could the taste of salt have some connection with our drive to survive? As if by instinct, we crave salt and understand its ability to sustain the human body. It also can preserve foodstuffs from rotting. In ancient times this commodity was so rare and precious that the Roman Empire used it as a form of currency for paying its troops, thus giving us our English word "salary."

If salt is so valuable to us as living human beings, then what craving for this taste drives us to the poison pantry?

Survival.

One of the most powerful fuels propelling us in the wrong direction is the instinct to save our own skin. But this motivation can easily be overdone. Heart patients and people with high blood pressure are warned of ingesting too much salt. Likewise, concerned people of faith must beware of their own taste for personal survival. Many of the same people who could join hands and ease the plight of the homeless and hungry are too concerned with their own hunger for personal salvation, and personal survival blinds them to the needs of others.

Even more unbelievable is the manner in which we see a few Christians fashion this personal obsession into universal doctrine. They reason, "Since God has prophesied the world will undergo famine, chaos, and destruction before the return of our Savior, there is nothing I can do to change anything without him."

> This attitude limits hope to the expectation of one's own personal escape—and perhaps in getting a few more people in the lifeboat while there is still time. In virtually every generation since the resurrection of Christ there have been a few believers who have decided their only hope for the future was their own personal escape. . . . Their eschatology had convinced them they couldn't make a difference in their world—and they didn't.[8]

We touched on this type of misconception in chapter 1 while exploring those who expect the poor to be "with them always" and so do nothing to help. But here we find a desire for personal salvation preventing believers from giving assistance to those in physical need.

You may remember one disappointed patriarch who let a taste for personal survival rob him of his future. Esau was the firstborn son of Isaac and had the opportunity to receive a fabulous inheritance. But instead, he sold it for a bowl of salty soup. The account in Genesis explains how Esau's brother, Jacob, prepared a delicious meal while Esau was out on an exhausting hunt. Instead of helping the weary traveler (his own

flesh and blood), Jacob demanded Esau's birthright in return
for nourishment. "Look, I am about to die; so what profit shall
this birthright be to me?" (Gn 25:32). Certainly Jacob was
wrong for holding his brother's life in ransom for his
inheritance. But Esau was equally at fault for placing the urge
for survival above the well-being of his progeny.

Satan tried this same ploy on the Lord himself. After forty
days of fasting, Jesus was famished. Satan approached him with
an offer of fresh bread. "If you are the Son of God, command
that these stones become bread" (Mt 4:3). We all know how
quickly the aroma of fresh bread starts our mouth to watering
and our stomachs growling. After forty days of abstinence, the
thought of bread would have activated Jesus' physical instincts
for survival. Satan wanted to use this to tempt Christ into
selling his birthright. But here the outcome was different.
Christ replied, "It is written, 'Man shall not live by bread alone,
but by every word that proceeds from the mouth of God'"
(v. 4).

The lesson is clear. We simply cannot allow our desire for
personal escape to turn us away from God and his plan for our
involvement in worldwide service.

Rather than lusting for the taste of salt, we are to *become* salt.
"You are the salt of the earth; but if the salt loses its flavor, how
shall it be seasoned? It is then good for nothing but to be
thrown out and trampled under foot by men" (Mt 5:13).
Rather than seeking our own survival, we must be willing to
lose our lives for Jesus. "For whoever desires to save his life will
lose it, and whoever loses his life for My sake will find it" (Mt
16:25). This is the exact opposite of humanity's inordinate
taste for the "Great Escape." You and I have a much greater
calling than mere survival.

Poisoned by Bitterness

Bitter is the taste of quinine, unsweetened chocolate, unripe
persimmons, or cabbage (to name but a few examples). We

sense it at the back of our tongues. In the raw, this flavor alerts us to foods that are not ready to be eaten or warns of things that do not belong in our mouth. In the hands of an accomplished cook, this flavor counterbalances or accents the other tastes. It's a tool for control.

And so it is in our "poison pantry." Bitterness intensifies some tastes and blots out others.

There's a meaningful reference to "bitterness" in the eighth chapter of Acts. In Samaria, Peter met a "certain man called Simon, who previously practiced sorcery in the city and astonished the people of Samaria, claiming that he was someone great" (Acts 8:9). When this man heard about Jesus and saw what the Apostles were doing through the Holy Spirit, he became baptized and "offered them money, saying, 'Give me this power also'" (v. 18-19). Predictably, Peter refused and said, "I see that you are poisoned by bitterness and bound by iniquity" (v. 23). This man of Samaria who had considered himself "someone great" had influenced the local residents with the fruits of bitterness.

From this account I equate the taste of bitter with those godless ideas leaders use to control other people. There are many to choose from in stocking a poison pantry.

Secular Humanism

One of the most bitter pills for numbing the mind of a believer is an adherance to secular humanism. What I feel is a clear explanation of this "intellectual seasoning" appeared a few years back in *Eternity* magazine. In summary: secular humanism is a cultural or intellectual movement, not an organized conspiracy. It is characterized by a climate of opinion in our culture that omits God and the supernatural, substituting self, science, and progress. It was popularized by the now-famous Humanist Manifesto I of 1933 and II of 1973.

In this century, humanism is often used as a synonym for "naturalism," the philosophy that nature is the whole of reality.

Historically, however, humanism referred to the study of the works of man as revealed in history, literature, and art rather than abstract philosophy or theology. The Reformation of the sixteenth century was indebted to the humanists of that era who had renewed study of the ancient biblical languages and texts. These classical humanists, almost all of whom were religious (Roman Catholic) people, should not be confused with modern "secular humanists."

In modern parlance, this term has replaced the epithet "liberal." A Sunday school publisher reports that critics of its materials two decades ago professed to finding them "liberal." Now customers detect "secular humanism." The term has found its way into the common language of everyday Christians.[9]

Related Bitters

Secular humanism is joined by other humanistic issues which can also leave a bitter taste in the mouths of Christian and non-Christian alike. I paraphrase these from an article in *Eternity* magazine by Donald Bloesch entitled "Secular Humanism—Not the Only Enemy."

Nationalism

Easy to overlook is the threat of nationalism. This sentiment enthrones the values and traditions of the nation or *Volk*, people. It elevates the national or racial heritage over the autonomous individual (as in classical liberalism) or the political party (as in communism). While secular humanism subverts the family by endorsing sexual freedom, "nationalism"—though posing as the family's defender—subordinates it to the interests of the wider community, the nation-state, which is adorned with a kind of mystical aura.

To date, American fundamentalism has been unable to

perceive or appreciate this not-so-subtle threat from the political ultra-right. This may account for fundamentalism's lack of credibility when it addresses issues that should command the attention of all people of moral sensitivity, including pornography, "value-free" sex education, and abortion.

Technological Materialism

We should also consider the threat to our value system imposed by technological materialism. Jacques Ellul has called this the dominant ideology in the modern industrialized nations. According to this worldview and lifeview, the prime virtues are utility, efficiency, and productivity. People who make no visible contribution to the betterment of society, such as the aged, the retarded, and the severely handicapped, are pushed to one side or even regarded as expendable.

Whereas many secular humanists are inner-directed and stress personal integrity, technological materialists are other-directed, emphasizing loyalty to the organization, whether it be the state, corporation, or union. While a significant number of secular humanists prize individuality and freedom, technological materialists encourage the dependence of humanity on technology.

Mysticism

Another bitter challenge to spirituality is eastern mysticism—that perennial temptation to turn away from the pursuit of pleasure and power in search of union with the Eternal. The penetration of eastern religions into the industrial West has presented a new alternative for tens of thousands of people. Eastern mysticism is usually a world-denying type of philosophy, but some neo-mystics stress immersion in the world, finding God in the depths of human existence. Whereas secular humanism celebrates the fulfillment of the self, mysticism often emphasizes the loss of the self in the collective unconscious, the cosmic process, or the "undifferentiated unity."

Eastern mysticism has crept into many of our churches and theological schools which are intent on recovering spirituality. It is also prevalent among many radical feminists, particularly those who are trying to reinstate the nature religion of witchcraft.

Nihilism

Perhaps, most sinister of all is the mounting peril of nihilism—the denial of all norms and values. Nihilism is particularly fostered by the technological mentality, which elevates efficiency over ideology and religion. Technocrats try to give technology a rational direction, but the temptation is almost irresistible to sacrifice ends for means. Moreover, a technology without aim or purpose, a soul-less technology, is more destructive than constructive. Indeed, the social agenda of nihilism is generally the overthrow of all existing social institutions and all norms. Nihilism ushers in the new barbarians, who are intent on destroying rather than creating, but they destroy in the vain hope that something new and durable will result. The dramatic rise in international terrorism is a manifestation of the unleashing of the spirit of nihilism.

Nihilists, like many mystics and occultists, are generally irrationalists, even as secular humanists and technological materialists are supreme rationalists. If the modern age is correctly characterized by what Francis Schaeffer calls "the flight from reason," it seems that nihilism, fascism, and nationalism may be greater threats than secular humanism to behavior and our sensitivity to the hungry masses of the world.[10]

I'm grateful to Donald Bloesch for the previous observations. But there is one more corollary to secular humanism I want to mention.

Social Welfare

Social welfare is eager to refine away the gospel from any charitable deed. This is part of the secular agenda which seeks to improve mankind through legislation, programs, good works, and social reform.

But the fruits of social welfare can often turn bitter.

Mary Clay is paralyzed from the neck down because of a spinal injury. She and her fifteen-year-old son have been able to continue living in their home, which is "bought and paid for," because the state of Washington has provided chore services. As a result of state cutbacks, however, it is likely these chore services will be discontinued. The consequence will be the breakup of Mary's family. She will be placed in a nursing home and her son in a foster home, and they will be forced to sell their house to pay expenses. Ironically, in the long run it will cost much more for Mary to live in a nursing home. After the money from the sale of her home is used up the state prefers paying nursing home payments to paying for chore services because "the federal government picks up half the tab for nursing costs."[11]

Just as "Simon the Great" was able to control the people of Samaria with his poison of bitterness, so the "great ones" of many lands have ruled with hard-to-swallow ideologies and motives. The Apostle Paul cautioned us to beware, "lest any root of bitterness springing up cause trouble, and by this many become defiled" (Heb 12:15).

During this inventory of the poison pantry we've tasted the bitter roots of human reasoning, the salt of self-preservation, the sour fruits of faith gone bad, and the sweet treats of materialism. Despite the fact these provisions have been packaged for consumption with misleading labels such as "light," "fat free," and "natural," we need to see them for what they really are: sedatives, narcotics, and poisons. I encourage every believer to strain out such destructive impurities when addressing the needs of the hungry masses waiting for our assistance.

With our senses purged of all adulterations, we're now ready to sample "wafers made with honey"—one of the staple foods for God's soldiers in the war against hunger.

The chosen people lost the land of milk and honey for the same reason Adam and Eve lost Eden, disobedience. It's the same reason Noah's contemporaries drowned in the flood, the tower of Babel fell short, Egypt lost her firstborn, Jericho crumbled, and the kingdom of Greece was divided among four separate generals.

FIVE

"Like Wafers Made with Honey"

I T HAPPENED EVERY MORNING AS SURE AS THE RISING of the sun. There on the grass and bushes was a white frost-like powder. All the hungry had to do was fill a small container and they had food for the rest of the day.

I'm speaking of the substance called "what is it" or "manna" by the ancient Israelites during their forty-year sojourn through the wilderness. Manna reminds us of God's solution to physical and spiritual hunger. It could have been dry, bland, and tasteless. After all, God had to provide for hundreds of thousands of travelers. You might expect this bulk food to taste like unsalted soda crackers. But instead we learn manna was moist and flavorful: "like wafers made with honey" (Ex 16:31).

God's plan for satisfying the spiritual and physical hunger of the world is as far above our own ideas as fresh cake is above stale bread crumbs. He who created the garden of Eden, every beast on every hill, and the daily diet of a traveling army of pilgrims knows how to solve the food problems we encounter today.

Then why did the manna stop? Why doesn't God keep on showering food from heaven instead of allowing part of the world to lavish in near gluttony while much of the rest of the world languishes on the edge of starvation?

We know God is not willing that any should perish (or go hungry)—(2 Pt 3:9). He feeds the birds of the fields and knows when even a sparrow falls to the ground (Mt 6:26; 10:29). Through the Apostle John, God says he wishes above all things that we may prosper and be in good health (3 Jn 2).

Where are the "wafers made with honey" today? In this chapter we'll examine some of the reasons God does not end the hunger crisis with edible frost showered over the earth. Then we'll look at some of the dramatic ways in which he *is* showering us all with physical and spiritual nourishment.

When Did the Manna Cease?

What plan did God have in mind when he withdrew the manna? Surely there was ample provision for its replacement.

> Now the manna ceased on the day after they had eaten the produce of the land; and the children of Israel no longer had manna, but they ate of the food of the land of Canaan that year. (Jos 5:12)

Once in the promised land God expected the Israelites to use his blessings to care for themselves. You don't need edible frost when you're dwelling in a land of milk and honey where one cluster of grapes is so big it has to be carried on a pole between two men (Num 13:23). All God required of the people was to serve and obey.

But what happened? The same thing that happened to the first residents of another land of milk and honey, Eden. They broke the lease. The Israelites forgot the God who gave them their land and began serving idols. They exchanged the laws of lasting prosperity for the "suggestions" and "guidelines" of short-term gain. In a word, they sinned. Not once or a dozen times as the occasional exception, but thousands of times as the normal rule. God said, "Don't make graven images," so they turned image making into a profession. God said, "Don't intermarry with the surrounding people," so they rushed out to take multiple wives from the idolaters. God said, "keep," and they broke; "remember," and they forgot; "live," and they died.

God warned these recipients of the good life, "You shall therefore keep all My statutes and all My judgments, and perform them, that the land where I am bringing you to dwell may not vomit you out" (Lv 20:22). And when they ignored his statutes, God brought the nations of Assyria and Babylonia as emetic agents to expel them.

The chosen people lost the land of milk and honey for the same reason Adam and Eve lost Eden, disobedience. It's the same reason Noah's contemporaries drowned in the flood, the tower of Babel fell short, Egypt lost her firstborn, Jericho crumbled, and the kingdom of Greece was divided among four separate generals.

So again I ask, why do we no longer receive manna from heaven? Because God has replaced it with something better.

During his ministry on earth, Jesus took many occasions to feed the hungry masses. But he deeply understood the transitory effect of such action. No amount of physical food can of itself bring spiritual enlightenment.

Jesus Christ understood this reality. The day after he fed five thousand people with nothing more than five loaves and two fish, Jesus explained:

"You seek Me, not because you saw the signs, but because you ate of the loaves and were filled. Do not labor for the food which perishes, but for the food which endures to everlasting life, which the Son of Man will give you."

(Jn 6:26, 27)

This admonition was too vague, too "spiritual" for some of the leaders in his audience that day. They wanted to know, "What sign will You perform then, that we may see it and believe You?" (v. 30). Christ seized this opportunity to explain why something more than physical nourishment is required.

"Your fathers ate the manna in the wilderness, and are dead. This is the bread which comes down from heaven, that one may eat of it and not die. I am the living bread which came down from heaven. If anyone eats of this bread, he will live forever; and the bread that I shall give is My flesh, which I shall give for the life of the world." (Jn 6:49-51)

History demonstrates that we human beings are more apt to forget God when we are well-fed and comfortable. Another sort of food was required. So Christ decreed, "I am the bread of life." But what kind of substance is this "bread"? How do we partake of Christ? And how does this nutriment solve the needs of a homeless woman in New York or a starving child in Africa? These puzzling questions are central to our understanding of hunger in the heart of God. Unraveling them will take a bit of detective work.

If Christ is the bread, then what we have to do is examine the central core of his identity to understand the ingredients of this loaf. It should come as little surprise to discover that Christ was born in the "house of bread." His birthplace, Bethlehem, means precisely that in Hebrew. Beth = house. Lechem = bread.

Who was born in this house of bread?

In the beginning was the Word, and the Word was with God, and the Word was God. . . . And the Word became flesh and dwelt among us. . . . (Jn 1:1, 14)

Here a Divine Being called the "Word" became flesh (at Bethlehem) and dwelt among us. Now the clues are beginning to fall into place. He who called himself the bread of life was previously known as the "Word." This title is corroborated by the Book of Revelation: "He was clothed with a robe dipped in blood, and His name is called The Word of God" (Rv 19:13).

Now it is clear. The primary grain in this "bread of life" is the "Word of God." Small surprise since Jesus spent much of his time imbibing the Scriptures and meditating on the thoughts of his Father.

But how does this intellectual understanding put literal bread in the mouth ce about this mystery is understanding "Christ in you." Just as Jesus became the living bread through the Word of God in him, so his followers can do the same. We'll have more to say about *how* this takes place on a personal basis in the next chapter. But for now it's important to realize the New Testament is filled with dozens of Scriptures about "Christ in you." Perhaps the key verse is in Galatians 2:20. Look what it reveals about the actions of Jesus *today*.

> I have been crucified with Christ; it is no longer I who live, but *Christ lives in me*; and the life which I now live in the flesh I live by faith in the Son of God, who loved me and gave Himself for me. (Gal 2:20)

> My little children, for whom I labor in birth again until Christ is formed in you. . . . (Gal 4:19)

These are by no means the only Scriptures which explain the indwelling of Christ. The Apostle Paul was inspired to write many other references to this divine mystery. "If Christ is in you, the body is dead..." (Rom 8:10). "... The life of Jesus also may be manifested in our mortal flesh" (2 Cor 4:11). We have "put on Christ" (Gal 3:27). "Christ may dwell in your hearts..." (Eph 3:17). To mention but a few. Most of the others are found in the books of Romans (especially chapter 8), 2 Corinthians, Galatians, and Ephesians.

The Apostle John documented this reincarnate process as well. "... By this we know that *He abides in us* ..." (1 Jn 3:24). Christ himself said, "I am the vine, you are the branches. He who abides in Me, and *I in him,* bears much fruit..." (Jn 15:5).

The Impact

What does this have to do with the hunger in the heart of God? Exactly this: where once there was one Jesus Christ on earth caring for the needy, now there are multiple hundreds of thousands, all of whom realize the importance of "living bread" complementing the mortal bread.

This principle fulfills a prophecy Christ gave to his disciples: . . . "I say to you, he who believes in Me, the works that I do he will do also; and greater works than these he will do . . ." (Jn 14:12).

As Christ's disciples today we can accomplish more because there are more of us. And unlike the 33 ½-year period when Jesus walked the earth, we have a High Priest at the right hand of God the Father serving as intercessor for mankind and steward of the Holy Spirit.

Where does this leave us in distributing wafers made with honey to the victims of famine, war, and poverty? Can we spin a cotton candy treatise on spirituality and walk away without even giving a teaspoon of sugar to the hungry? Hardly. Look at the extra strength this understanding imparts.

God is very much concerned about the disadvantaged. Why else would he sacrifice his Son for this growing group of humanity and all others who are spiritually impoverished? (Jn 3:16). "You shall not afflict any widow or fatherless child" (Ex 22:22).

The prophets loudly condemn the rich and influential who oppressed the poor:

> The LORD enters into judgment with the elders and princes
> of His people,
> "It is you who have devoured the vineyard;
> The plunder of the poor is in your houses.
> What do you mean by crushing My people,
> And grinding the face of the poor?"
> Declares the Lord GOD of hosts. (Is 3:14-15, NASB; see
> also Jeremiah 5:26-29)

God himself promises to care for the underprivileged: "A Father of the fatherless, a defender of widows, Is God in His holy habitation" (Ps 68:5).

Now we get down to the crux of the issue. HOW does the God of heaven care for the needy on earth? He doesn't come down and do it personally. What other method has he devised? The answer (which we've been moving toward all along) is revealed in the next phrase of this same psalm. "God sets the solitary in *families*" (Ps 68:6).

The best family to help someone in need is the natural, God-given family. The parents help a sick child. A grown child cares for the aging parents. Brothers and uncles help pick up the pieces after a local tragedy. But the next best family is one which possesses *Christ dwelling in it*. Such a family can dispense the bread of life and the Bread of Life.

These Christian family members are more than qualified, they are commanded to serve through admonitions such as:

> Pure and undefiled religion before God and the Father is
> this: to visit orphans and widows in their trouble, and to
> keep oneself unspotted from the world. (Jas 1:27)

> "Greater love has no one than this, than to lay down one's
> life for his friends." (Jn 15:13)

Therefore, as we have opportunity, let us do good to all ... (Gal 6:10)

"Assuredly, I say to you, inasmuch as you did it to one of the least of these My brethren, you did it to Me." (Mt 25:40)

Does this mean every believer should sell all and give it to the poor? Perhaps some should consider paring down to a more modest level, but uncontrolled giveaway programs weren't the answer during the time of Christ and they aren't the answer today.

Moses and Joshua proved, "You can lead people to the promised land, but you can't make them keep their promises."

Even if you and I had the power to dispense manna every morning and milk and honey every evening, we couldn't stop people from living the way of life which harms neighbor and brother, unless we could also provide love, joy, peace, longsuffering, kindness, goodness, faithfulness, gentleness, and self-control (the fruit of the Spirit as enumerated in Galatians 5:22).

Here is the enigma Christ encountered after feeding the five thousand and the enigma so many welfare and Christian relief organizations encounter in furnishing direct aid today. How do you help people meet their physical needs without reducing their motivation to help themselves? Goods without guidance only perpetuate bad results. We'll examine the balance between direct aid and evangelization in chapter 7. But my purpose now is to underscore the importance of "living bread" in every act of Christian charity.

The Voice of the Good Shepherd

"Christ in us" is recognized by many titles. One of them reveals a great deal about what we can do to relieve hunger in the heart of God. "I am the good shepherd; and I know My sheep, and am known by My own" (Jn 10:14).

When assisting the needy, unless our actions help reveal the voice of the "good shepherd," people will never find their way to the "green pastures" of lasting contentment.

What can the family of God do to help feed the starving millions of this world for his name's sake? I find many of the answers in the twenty-third Psalm.

The Lord is my shepherd. Sheep know and follow their shepherd. To make any kind of lasting contribution we have to be confident the Lord is our Shepherd. Many people venture out with little more than good intentions. They have no shepherd at all or, worse yet, the wrong one. This doesn't work. The best servants are those who are sent. A twenty dollar contribution given out of ignorance or guilt accomplishes less than a two dollar casserole sent by organized leadership.

I shall not want. Sheep give little thought to the next meal. How confident are you about your own personal needs? Without faith to see beyond the personal trials you're facing, you cannot inspire the single parent trying to build a new life on her own. Despite our wants, the Good Shepherd helps us understand there is hope beyond. We can live this day as if other things were more important, because they are.

He makes me lie down in green pastures. Sheep are always looking for for the greenest pasture. Are we willing to accept the voice of those over us and believe them when we arrive at a green pasture? Once there, are we willing to lie down and share it with others?

He leads me beside the still waters. Moving waters are exciting and challenging. They ask, "What's up stream?" "What's down stream?" Still waters are deeper, more settled, and boring. Do we have the patience to sit quietly with a bereaved friend? Or to make ourselves available for conversation night after night with our spouse and children?

He restores my soul. How messy does the shepherd get while cleaning and grooming a sheep? We who have been washed and refreshed by the Word of God are best prepared to confront the dirty stench of a homeless street person.

He leads me in the paths of righteousness. Unattended, sheep will almost always choose the wrong path. God tells us there is "none righteous, no, not one" (Rom 3:10). "All have sinned and fall short of the glory of God" (Rom 3:23). Yet despite this natural propensity, we can still walk in the paths of righteousness by humbling ourselves to follow his leadership. Those who travel this path are better prepared to meet the goals of local relief efforts.

For his name's sake. Our shepherd provides us with these benefits, not because of our goodness, but for the honor of his name and reputation. By human reasoning, one might suppose association with imperfect mortals would besmirch the name of the holy, immortal God. Not so with our loving Father. What should this teach us about being willing to associate with a so-called unworthy recipient of food stamps?

Yea, though I walk through the valley of the shadow of death. Sheep must travel through peril. We are not to expect a life in the open field of carefree mirth. Why should we be surprised by or critical of those victims who have fallen into life-threatening hard times?

I will fear no evil for you are with me. Like a secure sheepfold, God's presence is our hope and comfort. With Christ living in us, we can provide that level of encouragement to a runaway child or crime victim.

Your rod and your staff, they comfort me. Sheep have confidence in their shepherd because they see and recognize his tools. He uses them often and everyone in the flock knows what to expect. Do you and I exercise our Christian tools and armor enough to inspire confidence? Would a co-worker know you well enough to request your prayers for a personal problem?

You prepare a table before me in the presence of my enemies. Against deliberate threats, the shepherd provides for a normal feeding. The sheep are reassured and strengthened. Can a Christian who receives this type of support offer any less to a family whose livelihood is threatened by drought or illness?

You anoint my head with oil. Scrapes, bruises, and wounds need careful attention. The shepherd carries anointing oil for such emergencies. The Salvation Army and other volunteer medical units in your city and mine are always in need of helpers, donations, and blood.

My cup runs over. Full measure, pressed down and running over. Even a speechless sheep can utter thanks for such generosity. Would not an elderly widow in need of flour do the same?

Surely goodness and mercy shall follow me all the days of my life. Season after season, the shepherd delivers all that the flock requires. As recipients of the spiritual blessings of Christ for a lifetime, can you and I not contribute our physical blessings through a pledge campaign?

And I will dwell in the house of the Lord. Like a domesticated animal, this sheep knows it has gained the special favor of the shepherd. Attention and kindness are never far away. Having received these blessings, why would we withhold them from a fatherless child in need of financial support?

Forever. Blessed forever, can we sacrifice temporarily? Our shepherd did so for us.

Showers of Sustenance

Can you see the dramatic ways in which God is showering down his care on you and me today? Food is not enough. The earth had plenty of food before the time of Noah when "the LORD saw that the wickedness of man was great . . . and was sorry that He had made man" (Gn 6:5-6). Authorities tell us there is ample food for five billion people on earth today. The missing element is love—deep outgoing concern for our fellow human beings. That is the staple food item God most hungers to furnish. That is the food he is delivering through the living bread of Christ. Every hour of every day, on every continent, Jesus Christ is living his life again as a new creature within the hearts and minds of his followers. Each new son and daughter of God is another able-bodied family member who can help provide relief for the solitary fatherless and widow.

Pray the Lord of the Harvest

One day on the hills of Palestine Christ saw the multitudes and was moved with compassion for them, because they were weary and scattered, "like sheep having no shepherd." He turned to his disciples and said, "The harvest truly is plentiful, but the laborers are few" (Mt 9:37). Then he added, "Therefore pray the Lord of the harvest to send out laborers into His harvest."

Such a harvest would provide ample grain for supplying the "living bread" we have discovered in these pages.

Reading our next chapter could become the answer to that prayer for more laborers.

God is allowing all who "hunger and thirst after righteousness," all who have nurtured "a heart after God's own heart" to build their own personal temple to his glory.

SIX

Our Daily Bread, Butter, and Jelly: How to Feed Yourself

I ENJOY OBSERVING CHILDREN. Cute as they are, all children begin life with an absolute fixation on their own appetites. From eating and sleeping to playtime and entertainment, their total concern is "me!" This is as it should be for a newcomer who doesn't understand self or the world around. And things remain this way until we as parents instill some awareness of the needs of others. Then children begrudgingly learn to use the toilet, pick up after themselves, share toys, help with the chores, and get an education.

My point is this: children recognize their own hunger for immediate personal comfort. But they have to be *taught* about hteir hunger for a give-and-take relationship, service, accomplishment, and worship. Allowed to grow up without training, a self-centered child (in need of help from others) will become a self-centered adult (in need of help and control from others). Granted, all of us need help to some degree throughout our lives, but somewhere along the way we should outgrow our dependencies and become more other-centered—we must grow into the role of helper.

This type of growth requires a diet of mature instruction. Parents and guardians can start the process. But enduring success occurs when individuals take responsibility for their own education and training.

This chapter examines this process of nourishment and growth as it pertains to spiritual progress.

Appetites

You and I have many hungers. We hunger for food, comfort, love, sex, activity, recognition, success, and entertainment. We spend every waking hour *and* every sleeping hour trying to satisfy one or more of these desires.

One of the greatest appetites of an adult is the hunger for recognition, appreciation, and belonging. Many people satisfy this craving on the job. But what happens when the cupboard goes bare?

"Black Monday" was a grim reminder. Since the stock market crash of October 19, 1987, hundreds of thousands of workers have lost their jobs across America. Look at some of the results.

"I know guys who've been off alcohol for years," says one trader. "Now they're guzzling six drinks a day. Then they go home drunk and scream at their wives." Pace Health Services, an alcohol and drug treatment clinic in midtown Manhattan, reports that its caseload has climbed twenty-five percent since January 1, largely because of alcohol problems.

. . . Indeed, the layoff of 6,800 employees since 1984 at Phillips Petroleum Company has had far-reaching effects in Bartlesville, Oklahoma, the company headquarters. Last year's statistics (1987) from Women and Children in Crisis, a local shelter and counseling center for abused families, tell a grim tale: Requests for assistance shot up sixty-nine percent; women attending support groups for battered wives leapt forty-one percent; and the number of children in counseling groups rose seventy-four percent.[1]

Society celebrates winners. Anything short of that causes trauma and heartache. We expect initiative, drive, and self-motivation. God expects something above that.

"Blessed are those who hunger and thirst for righteousness, For they shall be filled" (Mt 5:6).

What can we do to help our children and ourselves advance beyond concern for personal hunger and into a new concern for humanitarian and spiritual hunger?

Somehow we must feel the need.

Planned Famine

In March 1988 at Pasadena, California 150 teenagers denied themselves food for a period of thirty hours. Their purpose was to gain some sort of understanding about world hunger by experiencing it themselves on a temporary basis from noon Friday until sundown Saturday. Only juice and water were allowed.

With stomachs growling, the students watched color slides of starving Ethiopians eating porridge fed to them by Christian missionaries. They played African games and created their own version of an East African village out of bamboo and palm leaves.

They also brought pledges of money. "It's just my way of helping out," said Darien Goehner, a sixteen-year-old member of the Lake Avenue Congregational Church in Pasadena. Before the fast, he convinced thirty classmates in his San Marino High School speech class to pledge one dollar each. Parents, neighbors, and friends also helped. The goal of the event was $30,000. Half of the money was to go to World Vision to support its nondenominational relief activities in eighty-five countries. The other half was for Harambee

Christian Family Center, another nondenominational group offering literacy programs, summer camping, and Bible studies for northwest Pasadena.

Fasting caused seventeen-year-old Kristina Beck to view world hunger with a much keener awareness. "I've been very fortunate, very lucky. I haven't had to go without food, without water," she said. "I have a refrigerator full of food. I have a choice. They [Ethiopians] don't."

"We're trying to help them empathize with people," said Patty Kelley of World Vision. "But there's really no way . . . for kids like these to relate to the hunger situation in the Third World." Still, she said, the weekend was one step toward helping them grow in their awareness.

Stop Hunger—Fast

This concept was patterned after an earlier project created by my friend Tony Hall, Chairman of the International Task Force of the Select Committee on Hunger, and congressional representative from Ohio.

"Stop Hunger . . . Fast!" was organized in Dayton, Ohio to stimulate interest in both domestic and global hunger. It too was a weekend fundraiser. Thousands of Dayton area citizens participated in a forty-hour fast in May of 1985. Pledges were collected for each hour they fasted. This project raised a total of over $400,000 in cash and food donations. Half went to local food banks and the other half to charities fighting hunger in Africa.

It is interesting to note that Christ prophesied his disciples would fast. "Then the disciples of John came to Him, saying, 'Why do we and the Pharisees fast often, but Your disciples do not fast?' And Jesus said to them, 'Can the friends of the bridegroom mourn as long as the bridegroom is with them? But the days will come when the bridegroom will be taken away from them, and then they will fast'" (Mt 9:14-15). Such a remark could also be taken as a command.

Weight of Inner Hunger

Another way to grow beyond self-concern is to see the end result of such action.

Walter Hudson once weighed 1,200 pounds. The contrast between him and the matchstick children I knew in Africa was overwhelming. He received national attention in the United States for his efforts to lose weight and become "normal." But how can you become normal when you weigh three-fifths of a ton?

Hunger for meaning in life drove Walter Hudson to obsessive eating. He never blamed his weight on medical problems. "I was addicted to food, the same way an alcoholic is addicted to liquor," he admitted.[2]

His mother would try to keep Walter on a supervised diet when he was a youngster. "But I would sneak off to the fridge after she slept," he confides.

Costing up to $300 per week, Walter's typical menu consisted of the following: for breakfast, he would eat a pound of bacon, two pounds of sausage, a dozen eggs, coffee, orange juice, six doughnuts, and potatoes. Lunch was three hero sandwiches, a box of cupcakes, and a large bottle of soda. At dinner, he was ready for two chickens, corn on the cob, and vegetables.

His body became so large all he could do was recline on his bed for most of the day with a sheet or perhaps nothing covering his massive torso. Hudson was approximately six feet long and nine feet around. Each morning he would give himself a sponge bath using a bucket, washcloth, and long stick. He hadn't set foot outdoors for twenty-seven years, not even to attend his mother's funeral.

Living in near seclusion with his brothers and sisters in New York, he continued to gain weight until a crisis brought him face-to-face with an appetite for change. In the autumn of 1987, Walter Hudson took a fall in his bathroom. Firemen, police, and the county emergency team labored four and one-half hours to dislodge him from this potential grave of living flesh.

"I felt I was seeing death. Face down, I saw I was in a world of trouble. I wasn't embarrassed. I was scared," remembers Walter.

"He was lying flat on his belly for four and one-half hours," said Robert Grams, the town's fire chief. "I did not think anyone could be that big. When it was over and we had him on his bed, he was so appreciative, he wanted to feed us." Instead, Grams went out and lost thirty pounds himself soon thereafter.

The publicity caused by this incident ended Walter's life of seclusion. Newspaper headlines proclaimed him "The world's heaviest man." Where once he had only one friend outside his family, he now was getting calls and attention from people all over the country. Comedian Dick Gregory took an interest in helping him lose weight. At last report Hudson estimated his weight at 700 pounds with hopes of dropping to 190 within four years. One of his goals is to walk outdoors: "I want to feel the rain on my face and to see my mother's grave."

I found it interesting to note the prominence of religion and Scripture in Walter's quest for improvement. His brother, Len, was a minister for a small congregation which met in the family's basement. Before his untimely death in 1986, Len helped Walter develop the habit of Bible reading. "It helped me keep my sanity and my temper."

Will it now help him keep his self-control? Obviously Walter Hudson is hungering for something to enrich his life. It has to be something more than food. That pursuit almost entombed him once already. His real hunger is apart from the flesh.

Bread of Life

In chapter 5 we saw the importance of Christ as the Living Bread of life (Jn 6:35, 48, 51). We learned "... If anyone eats of this bread, he will live forever ..." (v. 51). What could have more meaning as the ultimate expression of growth and maturity than eternal life?

But how does one partake of such bread? This question was perplexing to those who originally heard the command from Christ. "Therefore many of His disciples, when they heard this, said, 'This is a hard saying; who can understand it?' " (Jn 6:60). In fact, the issue became so taxing "from that time many of His disciples went back and walked with Him no more" (v. 66). And these were *disciples* who lost faith, not the general public.

So what is the answer? How do you build "Christ in you" through the bread of life? By feeding on the same bread that nourished Christ, the Word of God.

> How sweet are your words to my taste, Sweeter than honey to my mouth. (Ps 119:103)

> I opened my mouth and panted, For I longed for Your commandments. (Ps 119:131)

> And have tasted the good word of God. . . . (Heb 6:5)

> . . . Man shall not live by bread alone, but by every word that proceeds from the mouth of God. (Mt 4:4)

> . . . The words that I speak to you are spirit, and they are life. (Jn 6:63)

The results of this process are eternal life in the age to come and lasting accomplishment in the here and now.

But feeding on the Word of God is not easy. What can we do to make the experience more like the "honey" David enjoyed?

The 2/4/6 Club

Many years ago I heard a friend of mine, Pastor Ray Stedman, talk about a special group of men he had gathered to meet with him on a weekly basis. These men were not all members of his congregation, but were close friends who encouraged each other in their spiritual walk. He said his experience with those men was one of the most meaningful experiences in his life.

After thinking about it and realizing the need for such growth in my own life, I talked to my pastor. Dr. Ray Ortlund was interested. He expressed similar deep needs and feelings, so we met a couple of times to discuss the concept. Then we invited several men to meet with us. Some of the original group dropped out, but ultimately there were six of us who met together for more than ten years in a local restaurant. We called it the 2/4/6 Club, indicating that there were six of us, who met on the second and fourth Friday mornings of each month for breakfast. We met at 7:00 A.M. for approximately an hour and a half.

It was not a prayer group, although we did pray together. It was not a Bible study group, although we did spend time in the Word. It was a time of meeting and growing together, appreciating each other, and sharing our individual spiritual pilgrimages. There was no appointed leader and no agenda. We met to share experiences, to laugh, to weep. We rejoiced in our successes. We also shared and wept together over failures. Those meetings proved to be a tremendously significant experience in my life. The constituency of the group has changed now, and I meet with another group on a monthly basis.

During one of our times together, we decided each of us needed to develop a strategy for spiritual effectiveness. We agreed that in the month following we would each develop such a strategy and share it with the group. Though that happened nearly twenty years ago, I still carry in my wallet what has become a tattered yellow card. The heading reads: "A Spiritual Strategy for Maximum Spiritual Effectiveness." Over the years I have reviewed the list frequently and tried to keep my feet to the fire regarding the following six challenges.

Strategy for Maximum Spiritual Effectiveness

1. I deliberately place myself daily before God to allow him to use me as he will (Rom 12:1-2).
2. Ask God at a specific time *daily* to reveal his strategy and will for me that day.
3. Set and achieve a goal for personal spiritual development through reading one significant book per week.
4. Isolate a known point of weakness (spiritually), and work on it with the help of the Holy Spirit to correct and improve this weakness.
5. Make a study of several Bible people who are good examples—and seek deliberately to emulate them in their strong points.
6. Set up a measuring device to check spiritual development (quantitatively) and measure regularly.[3]

These six points have helped me immensely.

Paul relates the example of a group of Christians who worked together to grow in scriptural understanding. He says of brethren in the city of Berea in northern Greece:

These were more fair-minded than those in Thessalonica, in that they received the word with all readiness and searched the Scriptures daily to find out whether these things were so.
(Acts 17:11)

This was no small chore for the citizens of that day. Handwritten manuscripts were rare and valuable treasures. Only the synagogues, regional libraries, or well-to-do believers had them. Seldom could anyone find a complete set in one place. To check a passage in Isaiah might require half a day's journey from where they could read the Pentateuch (the five books of Moses). The readiness of the Bereans demanded teamwork and cooperation, to say nothing of a "hunger for righteousness."

Like loaves of bread, the Word of God is something you can divide and share. Speaking to the young evangelist, and his son in the faith, Timothy, Paul again writes: "Be diligent to present yourself approved to God, a worker who does not need to be ashamed, rightly dividing the word of truth" (2 Tm 2:15).

Peter has the same appreciation for the nutritional benefit of the Scriptures. "But grow in the grace and knowledge of our Lord and Savior Jesus Christ . . ." (2 Pt 3:18).

The times when I've felt spiritually impoverished are those times I've not been seeking the Lord in my own personal devotional life: getting in the Word, praying, and drawing close to God. The Bible encourages us to ask for our "daily bread." I hope you include the spiritual bread of his Word in that request.

Who is Partaking?

Gallup polls released a fascinating study. It is an update of their own landmark report ten years earlier on church attendance in the United States.

This poll gives you some idea of how Americans feed themselves on the Word of God. The signals are mixed.

"While the number of 'belongers' has declined since the 1978 survey, the number of believers has grown," George Gallup said at a recent press conference.

He went on to say that in view of the high mobility of Americans, the "distractions of modern life," and the apparent growing appeal of cults and non-traditional religious movements, "one might maintain that churches have done well to keep slippage to a minimum."

But is containment of slippage enough to prepare people for service to the world?

The surveys further showed between 1978 and 1988:

- Those who went to a church or synagogue in the previous

six months (other than for special holidays, weddings, funerals, or the like) dropped from sixty-seven to sixty-four percent.

- Those who said they were members of a church or synagogue stayed statistically even, changing from sixty-five to sixty-four percent.
- Those who met both of these tests, described in the study as "churched" people, dropped from fifty-nine to fifty-six percent.
- Belief that Jesus is the Son of God increased both among the "churched" (up four points to ninety-three percent) and "unchurched" (up eight points to seventy-two percent).
- Both groups were more likely this year to report a personal "commitment to Christ." That was expressed by eighty-three percent of the "churched" (up five points from 1978) and forty-four percent of the "unchurched" (up six points from 1978).[4]

George Gallup stressed that many Americans move easily between the "churched" and "unchurched" groups.

"Twenty-five percent of the 'churched' said there was a period of two years or more in their lives when they were not active in their church, and sixty-five percent of the 'unchurched' make a similar statement," Gallup said. "This is virtually unchanged since 1978."

The survey included 2,556 Americans eighteen and older.

I'm encouraged to see the increased interest in Christ and personal commitment to him. But I'm also distressed to see the ease with which we Americans pass into and out of organized congregations. One has to wonder if these "believers" are building any sort of commitment to the work of Christ as conducted by a formal church? In other words, are we professing Christ with our lips and denying him with our actions when it comes to the all-important areas of service to humanity?

The Need for a Congregation

This study would have us believe it's not important to fellowship with an organized church congregation. Such is not the feeling among a growing number of "Baby Boomers" returning to traditional churches.

Those around age forty "rejected organized religion on such a scale it was 'unprecedented in all of American history,' said Benton Johnson, professor of sociology at the University of Oregon in Eugene. Now the baby boomers, people in their late twenties to early forties, are *drifting slowly back* to mainline churches" according to the *Los Angeles Times.*[5]

This new appreciation for the pew is the result of many factors. For some it is a sense of family and security. One married woman and vice-president of a prominent advertising agency in Los Angeles derives familial pleasure from a particular weekly ritual at her local church. In a tradition known as "passing the peace," churchgoers greet people to the left and right of them with hugs and the words "Peace be with you."

"That feels real good when the rest of your life is dealing with aggressive people who have the attitude, 'What have you done for me lately?'"[6]

Other returning churchgoers seek the sense of belonging they felt in a congregation as a child back home. A minister to young adults remembers the time a parishioner family's van blew up while the family was on vacation. One child died, and two others and their mother were severely burned. Members of her local church supported the family throughout the tragedy and helped the disfigured children readjust to school. People miss that sort of friendship circle.

Many churches offer a convenient way to tap into current causes. At one church in Los Angeles, members can stop by card tables set up outside the building and sign petitions or volunteer to help shelter the homeless, curtail child abuse, or fight AIDS.

These sentiments help underscore one reality. It's easier to grow and feed on the Word while involved in a church. This should come as little surprise in the light of Paul's admonition in the Book of Hebrews: "Let us consider one another in order to stir up love and good works, not forsaking the assembling of ourselves together, as is the manner of some, but exhorting one another, and so much the more as you see the Day approaching" (Heb 10:24-25).

Heartfelt Desire of the "Man after God's Own Heart"

One man in the Bible is said to be a "man after God's own heart." What did he hunger for in order to earn such accolade from God?

The man, of course, is King David (1 Sm 13:14, Acts 13:22). Entire books have been written about his righteous exploits. He, himself, is the author of most of the Psalms. We could easily devote an entire chapter to this man of faith. But let me single out one ambition of this shepherd turned monarch which set a goal for all others who would seek to become a person "after God's own heart." Strangely enough, this is one great desire God never allowed King David to attain.

But the Word of the LORD came to me, saying, "You have shed much blood and have made great wars; you shall not build a house for My name, because you have shed much blood on the earth in My sight. Behold, a son shall be born to you, who shall be a man of rest; and I will give him rest from all his enemies all around. His name shall be Solomon, for I will give peace and quietness to Israel in his days. He shall build a house for My name, and he shall be My son and I will be his Father; and I will establish the throne of his kingdom over Israel forever." (1 Chron 22:8-10)

Yes, David made mistakes in life. But he always repented and showed his loyalty to God. Even after being denied the privilege of building a temple, David set his heart to supporting the task.

Indeed I have taken much trouble to prepare for the house of the LORD one hundred thousand talents of gold and one million talents of silver, and bronze and iron beyond measure, for it is so abundant. I have prepared timber and stone also . . ." (1 Chron 22:14)

Though denied the final fulfillment, he set his heart toward active preparation. This is our privilege today. God is allowing all who "hunger and thirst after righteousness," all who have nurtured a heart "after God's own heart" to build their own personal temple to his glory.

Do you not know that you are the temple of God . . .? (1 Cor 3:16)

. . . In whom the whole building, being joined together, grows into a holy temple in the Lord, in whom you also are being built together for a habitation of God in the Spirit. (Eph 2:21-22)

This understanding gives greater meaning and purpose to our daily walk with the Lord. Where once there was a lone individual trying to live a meaningful life, now there is a Spirit-filled temple waiting to serve the spiritual and physical needs of the world. Where once there was but a single widow, now there is a pillar in the temple of God. Where once there was a poverty-level family, now there is a temple filled with the treasures of God.

Throughout this chapter we have seen people who ate of the Word through fasting, through gluttony (repented of later), through fellowship, through church attendance, and temple construction. But they all had one thing in common. Each believer sought greater ability to feed the world (spiritually and physically) by ingesting more of the Word of the living God.

How fully are you partaking of this continual banquet?

Whether it's dollars for an offering or food in a bag, how many times have we held a small portion of God's collective answer to some problem without even knowing it?

SEVEN

Five Loaves, Two Fishes, and 15,000 Dinner Guests: How To Feed Others

W E DON'T KNOW HIS NAME, SO I'll call him Nathan. It was a warm and dusty spring day along the northern shore of the Sea of Galilee when the unexpected happened. Nathan had heard the grownups and his young pals talking about the carpenter from Nazareth who could heal the sick and cast out demons. Now this Stranger was headed to Nathan's part of the country.

"Nathan, quit playing with the goats and help us load things," called his mother. "If we're going to see the Master, we have to get an early start."

Now he was sure they were going to see the great Teacher. Excitement and curiosity mounted. Could Jesus really make people well? Was he the great prophet spoken of by Moses?

"You carry the food, Nathan." The trip was long and exhausting. And surprisingly enough, there were hundreds, even thousands of other people gathering to meet the Master. These crowds were beginning to look as big as the annual festivals in Jerusalem!

"They tell me he's tired of helping people and wants to get

away from us for a while," grumbled one old man with a cane.

"I saw him on a boat," a breathless teen reported to his family. "Jesus cut across the top of the lake by himself and got off in the wilderness near Bethsaida. Come on, we can catch up with them this way."

The gathering herd of people flocked toward the new direction.

"I'm hungry, Mom," said Nathan. "Can I have some food?"

"You can have a piece of bread, but I want you to save most of it for our return."

Rounding the last bend, Nathan was ready to stop. But he could still see the stream of men, women, and children spilling across the next meadow and up to the bluff. There the gathering mob suggested something of interest.

"That's him," called Nathan's mother. "There he is. Come on, let's move up close enough to hear."

Perhaps they had a pressing question. Perhaps they needed healing. Perhaps they were just curious. The Bible doesn't say. All we know for sure is the young lad was there.

By now the meadow was filling up with at least 5,000 men besides women and children. All Nathan could do was crowd in several hundred feet back. But even there he could catch bits of the Master's instruction and glimpses of excited listeners.

"It's gone! It's gone," shouted one ecstatic man. "Jesus touched me and my tumor is gone!"

Others who were healed pushed their way out of the crowd and back toward the lake in jubilation. A boyish curiosity drew him closer; occasionally Nathan could hear words of instruction or encouragement from the Master himself. "Don't worry about food or clothing for tomorrow. God who cares for the birds of the field will also care for you. . . . It's better to give than to receive. . . . A man's soul does not consist in the things which he possesses. . . ." and other such wonderful words.

By now it was late in the day and from around the other side of the bluff came a group of ten or twelve.

"Those are his disciples," called a voice from the crowd. "Maybe they can heal too."

But instead they seemed to be moving people away from Jesus and trying to disperse the crowd. Nathan came as close as he could in order to hear.

"This is a deserted place, and the hour is already late. Send the multitudes away, that they may go into the villages and buy themselves food" (Mt 14:15).

Then Nathan heard something which surprised him. "They do not need to go away. You give them something to eat" (v. 16).

"The Master's going to feed us," someone shouted, plowing instant furrows in the forehead of all the disciples.

Then one named Philip answered him, "Two hundred denarii worth of bread is not sufficient for them, that every one of them may have a little" (Jn 6:7).

This surprised Nathan. One denarii is the average wage for a day's labor in the field. Two hundred denarii could buy a small piece of property or boat! Who could afford that much for one meal in the wilderness?

But the more the disciples argued about how impossible it was to feed the crowd, the more the rumors boiled.

Jesus was as insistent as the crowd. "How many loaves do you have? Go and see" (Mk 6:38).

All eyes were looking about when Nathan remembered the bag of food he was carrying. "I've got something," he blurted out to one of the nearby disciples named Andrew. "Here, take this."

"There is a lad here who has five barley loaves and two small fish, but what are they among so many?" (Jn 6:9).

"I'll tell you what they are," thought Nathan. "They're probably my lashed hide when mother discovers I've given away everything she brought us to eat."

"Make them sit down in groups of fifty," said Jesus (Lk 9:14). So they sat down in ranks of hundreds and fifties (Mk 6:40). Jesus took the lad's loaves, "and when He had given thanks He distributed them to the disciples, and the disciples to those sitting down; and likewise of the fish, as much as they wanted" (Jn 6:11).

By now the disciples were bringing large baskets to collect

leftovers. "Gather up the fragments that remain, so that nothing is lost," said Jesus (Jn 6:12).

The Gospels don't tell us what happened to the young lad. Maybe he was one of those who were so impressed by this miracle of Jesus that they "were about to come and take Him by force to make Him king" (Jn 6:15). Or maybe he pondered the words he heard and the deeds he saw until Christ, the Bread of Life, could be formed in him through another miracle, conversion. What we do know about this lad is that he tasted a formula for feeding the poor—one we examine and use today.

A Formula for Feeding the Poor

Look at the steps this miracle of the loaves and fish followed. They provide a pattern for us today.

1. Maintain compassion. The disciples had just returned from their first official mission as disciples. They were tired and needful of rest. Christ was taking them off "privately into a deserted place" (Lk 9:10). But when the crowds followed them, he was moved with compassion to teach, heal, and feed them. Those instincts were always alive within him.

2. Don't be intimidated by the facts. Yes, it was true they did not have enough money to purchase food. Philip estimated 200 denarii would not be enough. How much was that by today's valuation? According to *Unger's Bible Dictionary*, "From the parable of the laborers in the vineyard it would seem that a denarius was then the ordinary pay for a day's labor."[1]

Even at minimum wage ($3.50), a fieldhand earns approximately twenty-eight dollars per day. Two hundred times that amount is $5,600. Very few missionaries carry that kind of cash on their day off. But even that sum would do very little for "5,000 men besides women and children." For approximately 15,000 people, our 200 denarii provides only thirty-seven cents apiece.

The facts become quite intimidating. We dare not let them limit us.

3. Use the available resources from those God inspires to help. The disciples saw what they didn't have. Christ asked them, "How many loaves *do* you have? Go and see." Even the most modest resource can reveal the way in which Christ has chosen to solve the larger problem.

4. Proceed in an orderly manner. Once the crowd realized the disciples had food, a riot could have resulted. God is not the author of confusion. Christ proceeded decently and in order by sitting them down in ranks of fifties and hundreds. He planned. He organized. He led. He prayed. No doubt this helped everyone get served in the least amount of time.

5. Follow through on the task. Christ could have left the scraps lying about in the wilderness, but he didn't. Instead he ordered the disciples to pick up all the leftovers for disposal. Perhaps they buried the remains or maybe they distributed them yet again to those who had long distances to travel. Unattended, they would certainly have been an eyesore and health hazard.

6. Learn from your experience. On several later occasions Christ asked the disciples how many baskets they took up after this miracle (twelve). The Bible records the number in attendance as about 5,000 men besides women and children. Quantifying results was apparently as important to Christ in his day as it is to a board of directors or planning committee today.

With this six-point pattern, we can now take a look at how to meet the challenge of feeding hungry men, women, and children in *our* era.

Maintain Your Compassion

Nathan probably heard Andrew trying to send people away, until Jesus reminded his disciples of the importance of compassion. God has a full-time concern for the needy. Literally hundreds of verses focus on these needs, from the first food in Genesis to the final tree of life in Revelation. God delivered Noah out of universal oppression. Abraham fled a famine by going into Egypt. Moses led this nation out of bondage and poverty. When the people of Israel neglected the needy, God neglected them. National captivity was partially the result of insensitivity toward the fatherless, widows, poor, and homeless.

Jesus began his ministry by quoting the prophet Isaiah (61:1-2):

> "The Spirit of the LORD is upon Me, Because He anointed Me to preach the gospel to the poor. He has sent Me to proclaim release to the captives, And recovery of sight to the blind, To set free those who are downtrodden, To proclaim the favorable year of the LORD." (Lk 4:18-19, NASB)

Paul admonishes, "As we have opportunity, let us do good to all . . ." (Gal 6:10).

Knowing we should have compassion is one thing. Feeling it and acting upon it are completely different matters. Many Christians have taken direction from the following passage.

> I have surely *seen* the oppression of My people who are in Egypt, and have *heard* their cry because of their taskmasters, for *I know their sorrows.* So I have come down *to deliver* them out of the hand of the Egyptians . . . Come now, therefore, and *I will send you* . . . that you may bring My people . . . out of Egypt. (Ex 3:7-8, 10)

Dr. Martin Luther King, Jr. used this Scripture frequently. Many in Latin America working in ghettos and barrios find great hope in it because of the confidence it inspires when they realize God sees, hears, and knows their affliction and suffering, and he wishes to come down and deliver them—usually by sending his servants to help in their deliverance through compassion.

But beware of wrong motivation. Sometimes our desire to

serve stems not from heartfelt concern, but from personal interest. For instance, the homeless deprive many well-off people of their sense of safety and comfort. One observer wrote, "Most of our strategies to help the homeless are based not on compassion, but on a passion for control."[2]

Do we simply want to get rid of these "inferior human eye sores?" Or do we really feel compelled to help?

Years ago when I first came to World Vision we used to reserve the bulk of our compassion for those in the body of Christ, his church. Today the organization is more open and direct in obedience to the biblical injunction of 2 Corinthians 9:10, 13:

> Now he who supplies seed to the sower and bread for food will also supply and increase your store of seed and will enlarge the harvest of your righteousness.... Because of the service by which you have proved yourselves, men will praise God for the obedience that accompanies your confession of the gospel of Christ, and for your generosity in sharing with them and with everyone else. (NIV)

Believers and "everyone else" need the compassion of God and Christ.

Don't Be Intimidated by the Facts

I am sobered by the words of my friend, United States Senator Mark O. Hatfield, a compassionate member of the World Vision board of directors since 1973. These remarks were delivered as a challenge to government, business, and religious leaders in several African countries during a 1983 visit.

> Next to the nuclear arms race, hunger is the most destabilizing force in the world today. Although we ought to care for our needy brothers and sisters simply on the basis of

spiritual commitment, even self-interest should cause us to do so. For, my dear friends, desperate people do desperate things. By the end of this century, sixty nations of the world will have the capability of building nuclear weapons. And in many cases this knowledge will be in the madmen who have nothing to lose but their chains. We live in a tenuous situation. We live on the brink of global suicide.[3]

As we've seen throughout these pages, most of the world is hungry. Yet, those who can be of greatest help are too often intimidated by the magnitude of the problem and shrink back into inaction.

Where did we get our attitudes and motivations? Like skin color and personality traits, we came by them naturally, from our parents and early reinforcement.

The first producers of world food, Adam and Eve, became intimidated by the challenge before them. God gave them a farmer's know-how in how to maintain optimum food production in an ideal setting. All they had to do was follow the program (dress and keep the garden). Instead, they allowed their own desire for more to supplant obedience and service. As a result, they were banished from the garden and forced to struggle for every meal. All because they became intimidated by what they didn't have (the Tree of the Knowledge of Good and Evil) instead of remaining satisfied by what they did have (every other tree of the garden including the Tree of Life). One of our jobs is to be aware of intimidating facts while firmly reliant upon inexhaustible faith.

Use Available Resources

Nathan appeared before the disciples with his loaves and his fish because someone in his family was concerned about hunger. One lad doesn't need five loaves or even two fish. I suspect this meal was prepared to be shared. And because it was made with love, God was able to bless and enlarge it with his greater love.

Here's a true story from Iowa. It illustrates what happens when one believer sees what *is* rather than what is not.

A grain merchant was respected in his small town community in Iowa. The church asked him if he would be the treasurer for the upcoming year. He didn't want to do it.

"No," he said. "No, I don't think I should do it."

They pled with him. "You're respected and we're in trouble financially. Won't you sit in and become our treasurer?"

"All right, I'll do it on one condition, that you let me handle *all* the finances of the church. But don't ask me any questions. I'll give you a full report at the end of the year at our annual meeting. But you dare not ask me any questions about what's happening." It was agreed.

It was a very successful year for that church in Iowa. Everyone enjoyed having the bills paid on time and no financial worries to fear. But the whole community was wondering, "How did he do it?"

At the annual meeting a year later, the once-reluctant treasurer gave his report. They had a balance. Every bill was paid. The missions giving had doubled.

"What did you do?" asked the pastor and leading men of the congregation. "Tell us about it."

"Well, as you know, I'm a grain merchant and you bring me all your grain from month to month. I've taken ten percent of everything you've brought me, put it aside and sold it for the church. That ten percent of the grain, which you didn't even miss, has made us a profitable congregation."

Whether it's dollars for an offering or food in a bag, how many times have we held a small portion of God's collective answer to some problem without even knowing it? That's why we all need a renewed vision to realize what Christ can do with our modest resources when we offer them in faith and love.

Proceed in an Orderly Manner

When it comes to large organized efforts for administering aid, my experience suggests the most effective tools have been and are non-government organizations (NGOs) and not-for-profit groups.

I know of one successful partnership with the United States Navy called "Operation Handclasp." This program uses government ships to carry surplus food overseas in empty bins as space becomes available.

But you have to be careful the tail doesn't wag the dog. Especially in locales where a national government is not present or welcomed. For instance, the Marxist regime of Ethiopia would not allow hunger corps workers to bring in supplies from the U.S. government but they did welcome emergency relief distributed by volunteer organizations.

In my mind the best "order" in international development is *Christian order*. To carry out development which does not potentially lead to a reestablished relationship with the ruler of all the universe is to carry out development that is severely lacking. Lasting development requires us to be tremendously concerned about the spiritual todays and tomorrows of people in need. (Even Christ prayed over his food before the miracle occurred). And that demands an understanding of how to transform teeming crowds into small, patient congregations of fifty or one hundred.

Fortunately, most Christian relief organizations maintain an approach toward development which lends a strong sense of purpose and order. Christian development implies a serious attempt to assist a community to become truly human, to live life in which there is economic, social, and spiritual self-determination for all. It has to do with the spiritual, physical, and emotional quality of a people's life. It involves doing something with whatever means are available. Development is people-oriented. It is a passion for helping men, women, and children become all God wants them to be.

The implications of evangelization for development are hardly as simple as giving a radiant testimony with each training session or including a full color gospel tract in each bag of seed. There is a time for every event, God's time. The secular experts in community development tell us in order to give people basic necessities we must begin with water, then move to food, and then to the production of materials over and above the need of the community so the community may obtain reserve resources. The assumption is that one follows the other. It is useless to plant seed if there is no water. In other words, every attempt is made to see that everything is done in its place and in relationship to the whole. In the same way, there is a time for each evangelistic action. There is a time to sow and a time to reap.

Cultural research also demonstrates that when the most well-meaning assistance is given improperly, it is usually viewed as "outside" and will often be rejected after the resource person has left. There are hundreds of rusting tractors and broken water pumps giving mute testimony to the best of intentions. Many of us who have been involved in evangelism can give examples that have achieved a similar result. The seed was broadcast, but the cultural ground was not adequately prepared.

I don't know about you, but I probably wouldn't be sharing my time, energy, and money with absolute strangers if it weren't for the "Christian" element involved in development. I appreciate the input here from my longtime associate Ed Dayton. He developed the following *Components of Christian Development* for lectures and courses we present in the United States and around the world.

Components of Christian Development

1. Christian development is carried out by Christians: people who have had their own personal encounter with the person of Jesus Christ, people who know there is something more to life than bread. The gospel contains more than the content of its message. We do not offer aid in order to evangelize. Rather, we attempt to meet the need that is before us.

2. Christian development integrates a new worldview resulting from the knowledge of Christ. This integration is done in such a way that it is seen as part of all being offered. There is a

wholeness to all of life. Outcomes are anticipated at all levels. In years past we have been accused of creating "rice Christians." Christian development struggles to avoid such an accusation by demonstrating how becoming a new creature in Christ truly makes all things new, including one's outlook on the economic and social environment.

3. Christian development comes from people who see themselves as enablers, rather than those seeking to impose on a people for their "own good." It adopts the stance of a learner as well as teacher. Christians engaging in development are themselves undergoing the same process. They are moving toward a more human existence and will learn new dimensions of existence from every community they are helping. This is not to suggest the Christian goes to learn of another god or to find a better religion, but rather when the gospel penetrates a new culture or subculture the Holy Spirit will have something to say through the newly formed church. We come as enablers of other children of God who have an equal potential to be Spirit-filled, God-led leaders of their own society.

4. Christian development plans to give the community an opportunity to confront the gospel of Jesus Christ and his claims. By attempting to see where a community is in the process of evangelization—moving toward a knowledge of the gospel, understanding of the personal implications, eventual confrontation with Jesus Christ—we gain insight into the immediate relationship between physical, social, and spiritual development.

Follow through with the Clean-Up Details

Once a meaningful menu of Christian development has been distributed via orderly ranks, some plan for follow-through and clean-up is required.

A useful tool for gauging ongoing needs in relation to gospel awareness was proposed by James Engel of the

Wheaton College Graduate School, along with Vigo Sogaard. It provides helpful guidelines for advancing Christian development in a sustainable manner.[4]

Engel Scale
of
Movement Toward Christ

No awareness of Christianity	-7
Awareness of the existence of Christianity	-6
Some knowledge of the Gospel	-5
Understanding of the fundamentals of the Gospel	-4
Grasp of the personal implications	-3
Recognition of personal need for a Savior	-2
Challenge and decision to receive Christ	-1
CONVERSION	
Evaluation of the decision	+1
Incorporation into a fellowship of Christians	+2
Active propagators of the Gospel	+3

This chart defines the starting point and tells what to expect next. It helps leaders involved in Christian development follow through in an orderly manner from one phase to the next. It allows recipients of development to quickly become coworkers themselves and begin supplying development to others in need.

Learn from Your Experience

A friend and fellow World Vision associate has taught me a great deal about building on past experiences in Christian service.

John Perkins is a black minister who grew up in Mississippi during some of the darkest days of white supremacy in that part of the country. His brother died in his arms from a gun shot inflicted by a peace officer. One Saturday night in 1970, he was almost beaten to death by a dozen highway patrolmen during a civil rights incident. But these experiences only drove John to apply the lessons he learned about Christian love to the needs of his fellow citizens in Mississippi. For years, John Perkins directed at least eight separate community service facilities in Jackson, Mississippi for needy individuals from the black and white community.

I particularly appreciated several challenges John issued at the conclusion to a chapter he wrote on reconciliation. His perspective motivates us to learn all we can about changing the unacceptable problems which exist in our communities.

1. What is the one needy neighborhood or community you know the most about? Close your eyes and imagine yourself walking up and down the streets of that community. What needs do you see? List them.

In other words, what lessons from past miracles in your experience can solve the present problems surrounding you today?

2. Now, drawing on the inspiration of what God has done at VOC (Voice of Calvary), imagine what ministries could be in place in that neighborhood ten years from now—ministries growing out of the needs you have seen in that community. What reconciliation could take place during the next ten years?

In other words, remember how many baskets of leftovers the Lord collected last time and how much good that same type of miracle can do today.

3. Imagine that those ten years have passed and your dreams are now reality. The time has come for you to write your own "Ten Years Later" account. Sketch out a brief outline of what you would include in your report. You might even include a tour of the neighborhood.

What miracles do you remember which serve as a vision for the future?[5]

One of the privileges of my ministry is the opportunity to teach the teachers. I have been privileged to be involved in a great number of international conferences aimed at helping local pastors gain greater knowledge about the Word of God. These have always been a source of continual surprise and gratification as these key Christian leaders express their appreciation for what they receive.

Kim Jai Ho, one of the delegates to the first conference for local pastors held by World Vision at the close of the Korean War, is typical of many such teachers. He told the faculty there, "We are, of course, in great need of material things such as our living commodities, shelter, clothes, and so on; but in fact, we are starved for the spiritual food, the Word of God. This conference, in this sense, is a kind of special feast."[6]

Here we see Christian brothers with a great appreciation for the food they received from Christ and his disciples. In times of doubt or discouragement, all we have to do is remember the ease with which we filled those twelve baskets with remains, and how willing our Master is to perform that same miracle again.

Most of our examples in this chapter have related to large relief organizations. But these six principles from the story of a boy's loaves and fish certainly apply just as much to one family providing a hot meal for a disaster victim or to one man sharing his canteen with a thirsty traveler. We'll have more to say about what you can do as an individual in the remaining two chapters.

Conclusion

What do you think happened when the young lad we know as Nathan returned home and told his village that his box lunch had served approximately 15,000 people?

What does it feel like to break a loaf of bread into larger, not smaller pieces? How do you cut a fish so both halves are bigger than the whole? You and I can't perform such miracles ourselves. But we can gather together our meager lumps of fish and loaves, place them in the hands of the Lord's disciples, then stand back and watch our Master perform the miracles for us.

I conclude this chapter with a short verse which my good friend Norm Rohrer used in his book on World Vision:

> Love is a basket of five loaves
> and two fish.
> It is never enough
> until you give it away.[7]

I encourage you to take what is not enough in your life, give it away on behalf of the Lord and see what happens. Perhaps your name could then be added to our next chapter.

I've met Mother Teresa of India and seen her in action. One thing that impressed me was her lack of being impressed by herself. How can someone receive so much international attention and still remain so humble-minded and dedicated to the service of others?

EIGHT

A Feast of Examples

WE START WITH THE APPETIZER. What follows is a feast of examples from people around the world who felt the gnawing pain of hunger in others and chose to do something about it themselves. Take up your plate at the start of this buffet line of inspiration and join me for a lasting banquet.

Appetizer

What could make a more fitting appetizer than a story about a master chef who became a waiter for the Master?

New Life and New Vocation for the Galloping Gourmet

Here is an example I particularly enjoy from Tom Sine, the author of *The Mustard Seed Conspiracy*:

The last thing Graham Kerr was concerned about was the kingdom of God. He was at the peak of his television career as the Galloping Gourmet. He was very wealthy. He enjoyed absolutely everything this world had to offer. And he was miserable.

Then one day, as a result of the witness of his newly converted wife, Treena, he dramatically encountered Jesus and his life was totally transformed.

He says that there was no way he could continue his very successful TV career once he had surrendered his life to Jesus. He explains that he had been intentionally cast in the role of one of America's leading hedonists and taste-setters. Everything he used in public, from the cars he drove to the cigarettes he smoked, was provided for him to create the desired image. He says the only thing he ever had to purchase was toilet paper, because that was the only thing he ever used in private.

And so, realizing it was impossible for him to be a model of the self-seeking life, and at the same time exemplify the servant life of Jesus, he turned his back on his career and even gave away his fortune.

Graham and Treena have a new career with Youth With A Mission. Their annual breaking-even budget is only fourteen thousand dollars—a gigantic step down from the lifestyle to which they had become accustomed. Unquestionably, the most important aspect of the Kerrs' new life is their new vocation. God gave Graham a vision of a way in which the waste of the wealthy could bring hope and self-reliance to the lives of the poor. The premise of this program, which Graham calls Project Lord, is that thirty-six Americans who save fifty cents per person per day by cutting back on waste, could support one microfarm project in Latin America.

Graham and Treena insist they have gained so much more than they ever gave up. Their new life in Christ and the opportunity to be involved in making a difference in the world has brought a profound satisfaction to their life they had never known before.[1]

Favela—Appetite for Change

Does Latin America need farms and produce for its people from such projects as Youth With A Mission? To whet your appetite even more for large helpings of Christian love, let me escort you to the slums of Rio de Janeiro. This city, famed for its jet-set lifestyle and carefree carnival, possesses an enormous need for change.

Behold a "favela." This is the name for hillside shanty towns which infest the cities of Brazil. Here slats, plastic sheets, tar paper, and tin take the place of bricks and beams. In greater Rio de Janeiro, more than two million people live in approximately 437 favelas. Poverty, hunger, and crime are their daily companions.

A powerful book entitled *Hillside Woman* by Frances O'Gorman tells the appalling story of what it takes to scratch out a living in a society that should not exist. With no sanitation facilities, water, or electricity, the favela would make an ideal home for creatures with four feet or six, not two.

Some of the stories about these people begin to stretch the definition of "human."

I came to Rocinha [name for one of the favelas] when I was seven years old. My father lost his job on the farm. Everything here was covered in scrub. There was a big waterfall where we used to wash clothes. I found it odd. I cried. I found the houses here just like the pigpens back on the farm. As time went on, I got used to it.

I had a baby who was born at eight months. At eleven at night I went into hospital. My husband hadn't shown up at home for three days. I went off, worried stiff. I left my sister taking care of my little daughter. I had the baby at five in the morning. At eight o'clock I asked to be released. The doctor didn't want to let me go. I cried. I begged him: "If you don't release me I'm going to run away from the hospital." Because my sister was a young girl. When you are alone here on the hillside they grab you. They do scoundrelly things. I was on edge. By ten in the morning I was already climbing home. I took a bath. I wrapped myself in a tight girdle. Then I went to work.[2]

From thirty-five different women, the stories of pain and privation seem almost endless; open sewage, no kitchen, seven people in one room, three jobs a day, crime, police brutality, drugs, gangs, shootings, unwanted pregnancies, sickness, wife and child beating.

Do these "appetizers" help you begin to feel the hunger in the heart of God?

Salad

Moving down the buffet line, our food for thought comes from a first-world florist who chose to become a third-world worker.

Approaching retirement age, Denny Grindal and his wife decided to leave their florist shop and fly to Kenya on vacation. After seeing the large game preserves, they decided to visit a small Presbyterian mission among the Masai tribe, a tribe of tall warriors who live by raising cattle, following their herds from one grazing land to another.

Not long before Denny and his wife visited the mission, the Kenyan Government ordered the Masai people to give up their nomadic life and stay on a government-assigned reservation. When the Grindals visited the Masai on their reservation they were shocked. The land was nearly devoid of grass and water. A drought had killed hundreds of cattle and thousands of Masai were struggling for their very survival.

Upon meeting Denny, both the tribal leaders and the mission representatives asked him to come back and help them. His response was immediate. "What can I possibly do to help? I am a florist!" He and his wife returned to the United States and their florist shop.

But God didn't let them forget what they had seen. Thoughts of the troubled Masai gnawed at their conscience. So Denny went to the library and spent several months studying earth-filled dams. Then the Grindals took some money out of savings and flew back to Kenya. They met with the tribal leaders and shared their ideas; the Masai responded by selling some of their cattle to match the Grindal's money. Together they worked to construct the first of a series of huge earth-filled dams. In one night of torrential rain the dam—three football fields in size—was filled. And they called a celebration.

In responding to the call of God, the Grindals inadvertently created a whole new Christian career for themselves, spending six months per year in their florist shop and six months with their new friends in Africa. In years of working with the Masai, God has used this couple to build reservoirs, dams, irrigation systems, and permanent housing, as well as start literacy programs, community health projects, preaching missions, and vegetable gardening.

The Grindals are an excellent example of what can happen when Spirit-led Christians pour the oil of concern over a garden patch of challenges and problems.

Main Course

Join me now for the main course. What follows is a succession of three examples from individuals who hunger for change. Their feelings, their actions, and their admonitions help define a staple diet of God-like care, nutrition that could benefit us all.

American Samaritans

U.S. News and World Report called them "the American Samaritans."[3] Dennis Carlson and Beulah Downing are a husband and wife team who have been working to improve the life of Ethiopian villagers intermittently since 1958. Currently, on this his fourth tour of duty, Dennis is serving as coordinator of primary health care for Save the Children Federation/USA in Yifatna Timuga, Ethiopia.

Despite the heroic efforts of several years, the needs of this drought-stricken country have not diminished. During the last crisis approximately one million Ethiopians perished. But much needed rainfall hasn't kept pace. Now relief officials estimate at least six million of Ethiopia's forty-six million people are about to starve.

During all of their work with relief camps and health programs, Dennis Carlson and his wife are guided by the conviction that individuals can make a difference. "The biggest mistake outsiders make is in saying, 'We've got the answers if you'll just do what we tell you,'" says Dennis. "We want to work with the people so that when we leave, the Ethiopian capacity is better for us having been here."

Dennis first came to Ethiopia in 1958 to apply his skills as a nurse. But after four years as the only "doctor" for 500,000 people, he quickly recognized a need to tackle the cause of problems and not merely their symptoms. Thus he returned to the United States where he earned a master's degree in public health from Berkeley. Then he went back to Ethiopia for another four-year tenure, this time as dean of the School of Public Health at Haile Selassie University in Gondar. There he taught many of the people who now form the backbone of Ethiopia's national and local public health service.

In the 1970s, Dennis Carlton served as a dean and professor at Johns Hopkins. In the 80s he practiced public health in Baltimore's inner city. There he met his wife, Beulah—a math teacher turned social worker. When the crisis hit Ethiopia in 1984, both were eager to answer the call for help.

Beulah complements her husband by working with approximately twelve orphan homes sponsored by Save the Children. Education is an important aspect of her work. In this hostile land education means life and death. Research has shown that if a mother finishes the third grade, her child has a fifty percent better chance of surviving infancy. Sadly, most children miss school to gather firewood and tend the cattle and sheep for survival.

After many long years on the job, the work of Dennis and

Beulah is beginning to pay off. They have constructed four-room health posts in fifty-two villages and one hundred twenty-five more are planned in the next few years. Their oral rehydration therapy, a regimen of water and locally grown grain which restores valuable body fluids in children, has produced dramatic results in those communities involved. Deaths from diarrhea, the number one killer of children under five during the last famine, dropped in one year from 1,400 to seven hundred cases. Through immunization the overall death rate of Yifatna Timuga has dropped from nine to one percent.

With a realistic combination of urgency and patience, much can be accomplished by people who share God's hunger for progress.

More Obligated than Liberated

Richard Riordian is a successful lawyer from Los Angeles who understands the force and limitations of money. Though his net worth is somewhere in the neighborhood of one hundred million dollars, he feels as much obligated as liberated by his wealth: liberated from want, but obligated to service. Despite long hours on behalf of his law firm, venture-capital operation, and investment banking concern, Richard Riordian sits on the boards of about two dozen private companies and public institutions. His own private foundation directs the assets of about ten million dollars.

"How do I reconcile living in a five-million dollar house with people starving in Ethiopia or East Los Angeles?" he mused in a recent cover story for *The Los Angeles Times*. "It's a little bit like this: If I sold my house and split it all up and gave to everybody, it wouldn't make a hell of a big dent ... I think what I'm doing [now] is helping the situation more."[4]

There's little denying the help he is doing now. Besides such high profile civic projects as vice-president of the Coliseum Commission in Los Angeles, he has also set his hand to the task of raising one hundred million dollars for the Archdiocesan Education Foundation under Archbishop Roger M. Mahoney. This money will be used as an endowment for the Los Angeles parochial school system.

Riordian understands the "pastoral letter on the economy" from the American Catholic bishops in 1986. They declared "the disparities of income and wealth in the United States to be unacceptable." He may not agree with every prescription from the bishops, but Riordan would like to reorder society's priorities to devote more to the poor "in an incremental, voluntarist fashion."

"The bishops' letter talks about 'preferential options for the poor.' But the big question is how do you fulfill your obligation? I define it as making the poor equal to the task. Every human being should have the tools to compete; that to me is a total religion."[5]

Such tools require education. Thus, in addition to his work for the archdiocese of Los Angeles, Richard Riordian has also established a program at the UCLA business school to familiarize minority high school students with management careers. Several years ago, he formed another foundation to put computers in inner-city schools in New York City, Trenton, New Jersey, and Los Angeles.

As a man-on-the-go in the corridors of power, Richard Riordian reminds us that riches and compassion can share the same agenda.

Passion for Compassion—Mother Teresa

Her approach is simple. Treat every person in need as if that individual were the Lord himself. I've met Mother Teresa of India and seen her in action. One thing that impressed me was her lack of being impressed by herself. How can someone receive so much international attention and still remain so humble-minded and dedicated to the service of others?

Recipient of the Nobel Peace Prize in 1979, Mother Teresa

directs the "Missionaries of Charity" in India. This Catholic order is committed to serving others "as yourself" and operates with 1800 nuns worldwide, 250 brothers, and thousands of coworkers in thirty countries.

"For me each one is an individual," she once explained about her service to dying indigents, homeless children, and lepers in India. "It is not social work. We must love each other. It involves emotional involvement, making people feel they are wanted."[6]

Volunteers play an important part in Mother Teresa's ministry. Not long ago "Pat" Brown, Jr., former governor of California, spent several weeks making a first-hand contribution to her efforts in order to learn more about the meaning of service. His reactions were reported in *Life* magazine in April of 1988. They are illuminating.

> On arriving, I went to the mother house of the Missionaries of Charity. Mother Teresa asked me where I was from, and I told her California. Then she said, "How long will you stay?" I replied, "About three weeks." She said, "Fine. You go over to Kalighat and work with the dying..."

This is a stark, open room for homeless and poverty-stricken street people from Calcutta who have fallen victim to life-threatening illness. Most are malnourished. Many are stricken with tuberculosis or worse. The purpose of Kalighat is not to cure them, but to give them a comfortable place to die with dignity. The facility has two rows of metal cots for about fifty men. On the same floor, separated by a wall, are the women's quarters.

> The next day at six A.M. I joined the other volunteers—we were about a dozen in all, from Australia, Canada, Germany, Ireland, Japan and the United States—and several hundred nuns at mass with Mother Teresa. Everyone sat on the canvas-covered concrete floor. The windows were open,

and the street noises were so loud it was difficult to hear the priest recite the prayers. At the conclusion of the service, Mother Teresa took a few minutes to speak to the volunteers and give them encouragement. Again her message was very simple: "Jesus is found in the distressing guise of the poorest of the poor."

My initiation to Kalighat was unceremonious. I just looked at what the other volunteers were doing and started to do the same.... The first task was bathing patients. The older, sickly ones needed help. When a man could not walk, we would carry him to a small room where the men washed. Nothing elaborate, just two cement benches with square basins built into the wall. We took off their clothes, soaped them and rinsed them with cold water poured from a can or a pitcher. For those in great pain, we used water warmed on a stove.... Diarrhea was common, and it was not unusual to have to clean up a patient after he had soiled himself. After doing it a couple of times, it became fairly easy. I kept reminding myself of Mother Teresa's words: "What you do to him; what you do for him; what you do with him (you do for Christ)."

I confronted death every day. Often all I could do was sit and hold a hand while a man's breath became shallower and shallower. Those about to die would be placed in cots at the front of the room so that they could be looked after more carefully. Many men would come in dehydrated and the nurses would put IV's into their arms to get some liquid into their systems. Often it was too late....

One older man by the name of Thomas had a gaping wound in his shoulder—the bones were exposed. He could only lie in a very awkward position. But he possessed great dignity. When he died, Sister Luke, the nun in charge, made sure he was dressed in a new shirt and pants and laid in a new wood coffin. She strung flowers over his body. Thomas then lay in the front of the room for the better part of the day.

I could not imagine that a president would be treated

better than these forgotten people. This is what got to me: the dignity given people who had absolutely nothing. What a world it would be if somehow this became the predominant spirit.

At six P.M. daily I would get into an old ambulance with a half-dozen nuns and some volunteers and ride back to the mother house for a half hour of prayer and the saying of the rosary. Mother Teresa was always there. Afterward she would speak to the volunteers with an expression of indescribable kindness and power: "Pray. Have a clean heart. Thank God for the gift of loving Jesus in the poorest of the poor." No hype or manipulation, no one asking for an offering.

A volunteer can just go to Calcutta, show up at Kalighat and find himself helping almost immediately.[7]

I was particularly struck by some of the lasting impressions this lady of mercy made upon Pat Brown. "To me she seemed the perfect embodiment of enlightenment: love of God expressed directly by serving the poorest of the poor. . . . Far from being overwhelmed, she transformed whatever she saw."[8]

Dessert

These "main course" examples have been pretty filling. What we need now is something light and sweet. Here's a story from a book by John Perkins with a "honey" of an ending.

A Christian organization which works for economic development among the third-world poor is the Institute for International Development, Inc. Chairman Al Whittaker, a member of VOC's (Voice of Calvary) Board of Servants, was an executive with Bristol-Myers and the Mennen Company when at age fifty-four he left behind his financially rewarding career to help start IIDI.

His career took him to Europe, Africa, the Far East and

other developing areas. Over a period of years he became increasingly uneasy about his career and increasingly concerned about the poor. In the fall of 1971 he heard a former missionary share, in passing, his desire to see the resources of the business community applied within the church to meet the needs of the poor. He talked with the man that very day and in a few months he resigned his job and was on his way to Washington, D.C. with no money and no staff for the ministry—only a group of Christians with a united vision.

Al describes the work of IIDI:

The thing we are really all about is setting up small businesses in developing countries as a way of providing jobs for the poor. We hear a lot about hunger and its related problems, but the root of the problem is an economic condition. People don't go hungry because there isn't enough food produced. People go hungry because they are unemployed or so under-employed that they don't have enough income to buy their food. That is the problem. In order to do something to prevent hunger, we must do something to create jobs which, in turn, provide income to buy the necessities of life.

The way we create employment is by starting small businesses. By providing certain resources for the people in these countries such as technical assistance and financing, you can help them become business entrepreneurs. In the past seven years we have been able to create over one hundred fifty businesses of all types.

We presently work in four countries—Honduras, Columbia, Indonesia, and Kenya. A field director and a small staff in each country work directly with the aspiring entrepreneur in training him, providing technical assistance, and making loans available to start the business. As these businesses develop they provide jobs and a new economic base within the community. All we ask of the people we work with is that as they become successful they help someone else in the same way we have helped them.

For example, Tito is a man in Columbia who wanted to learn beekeeping. A Christian businessman from Canada went to Columbia, showed Tito how to make the hives and how to take the honey and market it. He loaned Tito five thousand dollars to start the business and told him he could repay in honey or in cash. For about three years Tito sent sufficient honey back to the man in Canada to pay back the entire loan. During this time Tito was teaching others the various aspects of beekeeping. According to the last report, there were five businesses that this man had generated out of his original business.[9]

Motivating as they are . . .

. . . such examples sometimes cause discouragement and inaction. One would think the story of a businessman who helps other Christians create jobs, or the tale of Mother Teresa's pure heart, or the account of the reformed gourmet cook would automatically prod us to greater heights. No doubt they help. But there is still danger of gazing on such lofty paragons of virtue and feeling diminished or inferior. It's a misconception to think God isn't interested in our service unless we quit work for six months and move in with the underprivileged. Such is not the case.

These "spotlight saints" never set out to put themselves on stage and capture the limelight. They began by taking one small step toward an obvious need and continued.

The story is told of a kind-hearted woman who died. She had devoted much of her life to helping others by giving of what she had. Quietly, patiently, persistently, she designed and prepared lovely garments for others. Here a robe for an expectant mother. There a jacket for a child. Here a tunic for one of the men of Joppa. No doubt the "tunics and garments," "good works and charitable deeds" Dorcas contributed helped many a nearby family stretch their budget and eat a little better.

She used her talents and gave of what she could until she "became sick and died" (Acts 9:37).

But the story doesn't end with her death. Love and gratitude from her friends spurred someone to make a bold suggestion. Instead of sending for flowers, they sent for a miracle. Maybe the disciples of Jesus could do something for her! Hadn't there been many a wonderful miracle of late? And wasn't this woman deserving of their love and gratitude? Assessing the situation the disciples "... sent two men to [Peter], imploring him not to delay in coming to them" (v. 38).

When Peter arrived, "all the widows stood by him weeping, showing the tunics and garments which Dorcas had made while she was with them (v. 39)." He put everyone out of the room, prayed quietly and commanded the woman to rise. Dorcas opened her eyes, sat up, and created a house full of joyful mourners.

Such an example shows us many things. You can serve God with the simple tools at hand. Giving to others not only adds extra meaning to your life, it can even add extra length to your life.

My friend and co-author, Bob Larson, relates this piece of wisdom from one of his associates, Bob Hemmings, who says, "You are only remembered by the quiet, silent acts of kindness you do for others." People don't remember how well you did in the stock market. They might even resent the "things" you leave behind. But they will remember you for your little-known, unannounced acts of kindness. There is the true power and greatness.

In the case of Dorcas, it was the things that she left behind *for others* which prompted her friends to challenge the grave on her behalf.

So lest you become immobilized by the false assumption we have to "sell all and give everything away to the poor" to make a noticeable contribution, I remind you of this enterprising woman from Joppa.

From quiet service at home to boistrous work in the villages of Ethiopia, we have partaken of many inspiring examples. These help us to realize hunger in the heart of God isn't much different than hunger in the heart of a Christian—if that Christian is striving to partake of the "Last Supper" we discuss in our final chapter.

Where are the Josephs today? It took only one during the days of Jacob and Pharaoh to save the known world from famine. Perhaps God won't send another as effective as Joseph today. Instead, God may be sending thousands upon thousands of little Josephs, individuals trained to make small but deeply meaningful contributions.

NINE

Hunger's Last Supper: Will the Suffering Ever End?

I T WOULD CERTAINLY BE EASY TO GIVE UP on the issue of world hunger. Since writing some of the earlier chapters I have learned of the mass slaughter of tens of thousands of innocent civilians in the African nation of Burundi. This is leading to devastating hunger and deprivation in the region (as those involved in that tribal warfare fully intend). Killer earthquakes have struck eastern India and Pakistan. Drought in the midwestern region of the United States has escalated into what government officials call "the worst disaster on record." Problems continue to mount. So the question: Will there ever be an end to hunger and suffering?

In the first chapter of this book I gave you a hypothetical invitation to a "surprise" banquet on behalf of world hunger. There we changed the menu to offer a better taste of world conditions.

Here now is your invitation to yet another banquet. The last one mentioned in Scripture, its purpose is to celebrate the end of world hunger. But this banquet isn't hypothetical. It *will* take place. And like all well-planned events, it is set for a date in the future.

Anyone may receive an invitation. But it has to be "confirmed" in advance to be valid.

The banquet I refer to is the marriage supper of Christ. Now before you dismiss this future, spiritual event as having little or no relevance to the present, physical problems of hunger, consider a few of the realities behind its symbolism.

This everlasting union with our Savior offers hope.

> "Blessed are those who are called to the marriage supper of the Lamb!" (Rv 19:9)

> And the Spirit and the bride say, "Come!" And let him who hears say, "Come!" And let him who thirsts come. And whoever desires, let him take the water of life freely. (Rv 22:17)

No matter what the ravages of reality today, God is promising a better life in the ages beyond—one filled with abundance, joy, and satisfaction. For millennia this has given so many—and us today—a purpose to strive for even in the face of adversity and heartache.

But this invitation to the marriage supper was never intended, nor is it now, as an excuse to accept deplorable conditions we can change through simple planning, sacrifice and hard work. To confirm our invitation we have to dedicate ourselves to a life of Godly service. The source for this mandate comes from the Word of God.

> " 'Therefore go into the highways, and as many as you find, invite to the wedding.'
>
> "So those servants went out into the highways and gathered together all whom they found, both bad and good. And the wedding hall was filled with guests.
>
> "But when the king came in to see the guests, he saw a man there who did not have on a wedding garment.
>
> "So he said to him, 'Friend, how did you come in here

without a wedding garment?' And he was speechless." (Mt 22:9-12)

And there shall by no means enter it [the holy city of the bride] anything that defiles, or causes an abomination or a lie, but only those who are written in the Lamb's Book of Life. (Rv 21:27)

Being properly attired and written in the Lamb's Book of Life is what makes God's promise for the future so meaningful today. This offer reminds us that *what we do today really does matter*. Those with an abundance of possessions, wealth, and food cannot turn their backs on the needy without risking their own invitation to the marriage supper. Those in need can take what little they have, use it to serve and to share (often improving their own lot in life during the process) and rejoice in the feast to come.

When this wedding supper will come is one of those things known only by the Father in heaven (Mt 24:36). But two things are sure. If it happens in our lifetime, we need to make certain our names are written in the Book of Life. And if it happens *after* our lifetime, we need to make certain our names are written in the Book of Life.

What does it take to place your name in the Book of Life?

So a book of remembrance was written before Him for those who fear the Lord and who meditate on His name. (Mal 3:16)

But are fear and meditation enough?

. . . Help these women who *labored* with me in the gospel, with Clement also, and the rest of my fellow *workers,* whose names are in the Book of Life. (Phil 4:3)

Here we find fellow workers, laboring in the gospel. This is our quill for making an entry in the Book of Life. Unceasing labor and work for God.

Does this mean we all have to join the formal ministry or work for a relief organization? Aren't there other ways to labor for God?

Gene Thomas, formerly a staff member with InterVarsity Christian Fellowship and now a businessman in Boulder, Colorado, offered a useful suggestion in *Christianity Today*.

A girl recently said to me, "If I go and become a bookkeeper, I don't know if that's going to be satisfying or not."

I said to her, "Would it be worth it if God sent you there and in the course of your lifetime just one person was brought into the kingdom by your being there?"

She thought a bit, and said, "I think it might be worth it."

People who are willing to have a vision of the value of human life can be sent to some truly difficult place, invest their lives in something, and really know that it is worthwhile.

... If the significance has to be in terms of numbers, then I don't think people are going to do it. We have to help kids re-evaluate their world, and develop a completely different perspective about what we believe about the value of one human life.[1]

Three R's

Another way to become inscribed in the Book is by means of the three R's. This concept was developed by my friend, John Perkins whom we met in an earlier chapter. The three R's are tools for effecting change in the areas of poverty and hunger. They are **R**elocation, **R**econciliation, and **R**edistribution.[2]

Relocation means the removal of one's self from the normal "good life" to the center of a need. We saw this so dramatically in our last chapter. The Grindals were willing to relocate to

Kenya; Beulah and Dennis Carlton to Ethiopia; Mother Teresa to the streets of Calcutta.

Reconciliation is the power to make people compatible once again. John Perkins had to be reconciled himself with both his black brothers of Mississippi and the whites who drove him from the state. This process is needed toward people and toward God. It takes commitment and work.

Redistribution is the actual transfer of goods or services from areas of surplus to areas of need. Moving things is simple. But we have to place this last on the list of three R's. Nothing can be moved till someone has relocated (their center of interest if not their very person) and achieved reconciliation.

To drive this threefold miracle, John Perkins recommends "voluntary oppression." This is the willful subjection of one's self for the betterment of others. It's by no means a popular notion. But it is scriptural.

> Moses . . . chose to be mistreated along with the people of God rather than to enjoy the pleasures of sin for a short time. He regarded disgrace for the sake of Christ as of greater value than the treasures of Egypt, because he was looking ahead to his reward. (Heb 11:24-26, NIV)

> For you know the grace of our Lord Jesus Christ, that though He was rich, yet for your sakes He became poor, that you through His poverty might become rich. (2 Cor 8:9)

Think of the implications. Even a seemingly ordinary life can become part of the labor of God if we hold that purpose in our heart. Driving a truck, raising children, answering the phone: any of these and a multitude of other actions can be performed with an attitude which can place a mark in our favor in the Book of Life. The more we act on this vision, the closer we come toward confirming our invitation to the wedding supper of Christ.

My Food

One time when the disciples went away to find food, they came back and wondered why Christ didn't seem hungry. "My food is to do the will of Him who sent Me, and to finish His work," he told them (Jn 4:34). Jesus drew physical energy by advancing the work of the God of physical creation.

Have you ever become so involved in a service project for a friend or associate you didn't even realize you'd worked through meal time? I've seen many a group become so involved in painting a room or preparing a shipment for overseas relief that no one even missed the meal.

On the other side of the coin, I've seen people (myself included) become so concerned about personal needs and "getting my share" that nothing was quite good enough. When people think they deserve the finest, not even the finest can escape criticism. "My filet mignon was a bit tough and too well-done."

We can't end hunger in this life. But we can end its grip on our heart. When those with enough to share have the heart to share, the needy will benefit. When those in need also hunger and thirst for righteousness, they can be filled with the same hope that strengthened our elder brother, Jesus, during his forty-day fast, and his torture and crucifixion.

Unalterably Intertwined

I believe the completion of the Great Commission and the commitment to helping hungry people are unalterably intertwined. Further, I see the requirement for a synthesis, rather than a dichotomy, of evangelism and development if we are to fulfill Christ's Great Commission and obey his great commandment among those who have yet to know him.

Bob Pierce, the founder of World Vision, believed it was wrong to separate social action from personal evangelism.

Our Lord preached the gospel of the kingdom, and that's social. The same word in both Hebrew and Greek for righteousness can be translated "*justice*": "Seek ye first the kingdom of God and his *justice* . . ."; or "blessed are they that hunger and thirst after *justice.*" Or the strongest one of all, "I am not ashamed of the gospel of Christ for it is the power of God unto salvation, unto every one who believes, to the Jew first and also to the Greek. For in the gospel is the *justice* of God revealed."

I also believe that in order to gain the attention of people who are hungry, it is not enough to stand with a bit of philosophy. Jesus said, "When you see a man hungry and cold, don't just say to him, be fed and be clothed." It's just as much the gospel of Jesus Christ that these men, whom we want to hear what we have to say, should be fed and clothed; and it is as truly expressed in the New Testament as many of the other doctrines we hold so dear.[3]

Without food, people lose their ability to understand God, much less respond. Without a home how can they appreciate God's offer of heaven? Too busy scraping together food, how can they receive the Word of God? With empty stomachs, how can their hearts be full of the love of God?

Wanted: Another Joseph

What we need is another Joseph. This patriarch faithfully endured betrayal at the hands of his brothers and ultimately dedicated himself to the task of turning his prison into a breadbasket which saved those same brothers (and numerous whole nations) from starvation.

You remember the story. It's recounted in great detail in the Book of Genesis, chapters 39 through 47. Joseph is hated by his eleven brothers because he was "daddy's favorite." They sell him into slavery and he is carried to Egypt. Falsely accused of abusing his master's wife, he finds himself in the dungeon for three long years. Yet he never loses his respect for and obedience to God. Favored by God with the ability to interpret dreams, and called out of prison to explain a dream to Pharaoh, he foretells seven years of plenty followed by seven years of famine. Then Pharaoh rewards him with the responsibility of managing the surplus years to offset the shortfall. Finally he is confronted by his brothers in need of food.

I appreciate the dramatic climax which occurred at another great banquet in history: the meal where Joseph revealed himself to his brothers, not in a spirit of revenge, but reconciliation. Here was a classic "Three R plan": relocation (to the land of Egypt), reconciliation (with hate-filled brothers), and redistribution (from seven years of plenty in Egypt to seven years of famine in other lands).

Where are the Josephs today? It took only one during the days of Jacob and Pharaoh to save the known world from famine. Perhaps God won't send another as effective as Joseph today. Instead, God may be sending thousands upon thousands of little Josephs, individuals trained to make small but deeply meaningful contributions.

What You Can Do

As part of this small army of Josephs, there is much you can do to address the needs of hunger.

Write to your congressman. It's amazing what an avalanche of power one tiny snowflake can start. James Dobson, founder of "Focus on the Family," and a good friend of mine, can make one request on the radio for letters to Washington and a hundred thousand people respond. What would your reaction be to a back-bending sack of mail on one issue? Not all of the legislators are disinterested bureaucrats. Congressman Tony Hall, Chairman of the Sub-committee on Hunger, whom I quoted in chapter 6, is a Christian and fellow believer. I know he appreciates all the letters he can get as support for these ideals. (His address is: Tony Hall, 2448 Rayburn House Office Bldg., Washington, D.C. 20515.)

Prayer burden: Pray for and create an action plan for renewal and revival at home, in the church, with your neighbors, and in the community.

Tell your children. We feed them everyday with physical nourishment. Why not feed them every week, month, or year with spiritual nourishment about our responsibility toward those who live without?

Thanksgiving: Why not take five minutes out of your family Thanksgiving celebration to talk about world hunger? Make times of celebration also times of sober reflection on the fact that we are part of a hurting society.

Grace at the table: Oftentimes I pray in a blessing, "Help us, Lord, to be conscious of those whom we serve who have so very little and we have so very much." It's profitable at home with your family or out in larger gatherings.

Share your agenda with those who suffer.

Here's something of value I found it in a public service print advertisement produced by the Ad Council of America and printed in *Newsweek*.

But think about it for a minute. If we all gave just five hours a week to the causes we are about, it would be like mobilizing a force of more than 20 million full-time volunteers. If we all gave just five percent of what we earn, it would come to 175 billion dollars a year.... One person may not be able to make that much difference. But 200 million people can make all the difference in the world.

It's been said before, but once you see it in action, you cannot deny the power of another simple reality. "Our greatest gift is the gift of hope." You and I have realistic hope for a square meal tomorrow, maybe even a restaurant meal the day after. Think what it would mean to have no such hopes. It may be hard for you to imagine, but the promise of hope for tomorrow that you and I can deliver to these people is actually better than a seven-course meal. These sufferers are intelligent and realize one meaningful plan toward a steady food supply is better than several temporary feasts.

There'll never be an end to hunger. "The poor you have with you always." But that doesn't excuse us from extending our hand to help them. I remember Bob Pierce's comment, "Simply because I cannot help everybody in the world doesn't mean I can't help somebody." Simply because I can't do everything doesn't mean I can't do something. We have to leave the final outcome to God.

The Heart of God

Throughout these chapters we've spent a great deal of time examining hunger in the heart of God. Our primary focus has been on hunger. But equally important is the *heart* of God. What is it like? For what does God's heart hunger?

The meaning of "heart" is not limited to the physical organ which pumps blood through the circulatory system, else God would not possess one. But we know he does. "Heart" as we know it from the Bible means the center of emotion, the mind, the strength, the central essence. This God possesses in abundance. Unfortunately, the first place we read about the heart of God, it is grieved. "And the Lord was sorry that He had made man on the earth, and He was grieved in His heart" (Gn 6:5).

Because God has told us ". . . His invisible attributes are clearly seen, being understood by the things that are made..." (Rom 1:20), I understand the heart of God by three main revelations, his creation, his Word, and his Son.

The Heart of God through His Creation

Entire books have been written to prove our universe is the handiwork of God and not the footwork of fate. So rather than trying to duplicate these accomplishments in one or two pages, let me proceed from my own personal conviction. When I look at the reliability of the heavens, the sun, the moon, and the stars in all their cycles, I see a God of precision. And through these miracles, he provides us with food, shelter, clothing, and companionship. Granted, there are thistles, thorns, and adversaries to contend with, but even these keep us mindful of our dependence upon the heart of a supreme giver.

Step outside on a clear night. Pick up a stone from the ground and examine it by starlight. Imagine, if you can, how those distant stars may have come from the same matter you're holding. Look about for a "shooting star" and toss the rock at it. Your chance of hitting that meteor are about as good as your ability to comprehend the mind and heart of the Creator who made both stone and star. But unlike the falling rock, God will bless our efforts to think on him.

Living plants, animals, and fellow human beings: all were created to grow, interact with one another, and reproduce after their own kind. Here is incredible design and order. I feel the presence of a heart which wants to cherish and share.

The Heart of God through His Word

Since I know there is a Creator, it only makes sense he would pass down instructions to his creation in some permanent fashion. The book we know as the Bible is the oldest continuous record of human history in existence. Fragments of other writing may exist from some supposedly earlier time, but they do not link up with any cohesive work still in existence today. The Bible was written over a period of one thousand years with same heart. It has survived in its present form nearly two thousand years. It contains predictions, many of which have already come to pass, many others of which are unfolding before our very eyes. This book of books explains the origin of us humans, gives usable guidelines for our actions today, and foretells our ultimate destiny. No other so-called sacred writing can make such claims. Some, such as the Koran, or the Book of Mormon, have been around for many years. But they were written much later than the Bible, contain no verifiable prophecies, and have not received the harmonious contribution of later authors.

The Holy Bible stands as the undisputed revelation of God to his creation. In it we see his mind, his heart, and his soul. Through one of the earliest chapters he implores you and me, "Oh, that they had such a heart in them that they would fear Me and always keep all My commandments, that it might be well with them and with their children forever!" (Dt 5:29).

The Heart of God through His Son

"If you had known Me, you would have known My Father..." Jesus told his disciples in John 14:7. He went even further in verse 9 by saying, "He who has seen Me has seen the Father." Through the pages of the Bible, and through the lives of true Christians, I have seen the Father.

God's heartfelt desire was to give mankind the bread of everlasting life. "For God so loved the world that He *gave* His only begotten Son, that whoever believes in Him should not perish but have everlasting life" (Jn 3:16).

Incredible as it may seem, this God who owns everything, this God who is supreme over all other beings, wants to place the needs of you and me above his own. He wants to give us eternal life (at the expense of his dearest possession, Jesus Christ) and share his possessions. That, my dear reader, demands a heart much larger than anything you or I can envision. We can only accept this offer in humility and faith.

God's heart is just, yet merciful. He knows we deserve the

death penalty, but sent his Son in our stead—as long as we agree to live as his Son would live to compensate him for the loss.

God's heart is generous, yet loyal. He is willing to share his creation. But he expects all who receive this gift to abide by the rules of the realm.

The more you look into the heart of God, the more you see. He's a Worker who created the day of rest. He's the Shepherd who invented sheep. He's a King who understands the role of slave. He's a Father who wants you as his child.

This is but part of the picture. Indeed Paul was right when he said, "we see through a glass darkly" (1 Cor 13:12 KJV). But you can see more about God and his heart if you follow a simple formula given by Jesus. "Blessed are the pure in heart, For they shall see God" (Mt 5:8). Purify your heart through the pure Word of God and you will understand things unimaginable about the God of imagination and reality.

As we know something more about the heart of God, can we appreciate more fully the hunger he experiences?

Is Jesus Lord in Your Country?

Let me introduce you to a fresh-faced little girl whom my colleague, Bill Newell, met in Ethiopia. She wasn't one of the famine victims. In fact she had recently received a feast of understanding about our Lord Jesus Christ.

Bill walked into one of the camps and discovered a fifteen-year-old girl writing in the sand. "Oh, I see you know English," was Bill's reaction to the familiar characters in the unfamiliar soil.

"Yes," replied the girl.

"Let's see what you've written here. 'Jesus is Lord.' Oh, that's wonderful. Does that mean he is Lord in your life?"

"Oh, yes indeed," said the girl with a smile. "Where do you come from?"

"Canada," said Bill.

"Is Jesus Lord in your country?" asked the girl.

Here's the part of the story I never have forgotten. Bill was

154 / *Hunger in the Heart of God*

forced to give a reply you and I would have to use if we are honest with ourselves and our Lord. "No, he really isn't Lord in my home country."

I can only imagine the look on the young girl's face.

Bill Newell said he never forgot the sting of that pointed lesson. We go to faraway countries to spread the good news of Christ and his love, and to do good works in his name. Yet we really have to confess that Christ isn't Lord of our own nation. If people lose confidence in the heart of our country, it's a short step for them to lose confidence in our hearts.

Personal Observations

I confess these observations are made by someone who has never faced starvation. I don't know what it feels like to become so weak I cannot stand or focus my eyes clearly. I've never had my body start dissolving its own muscle and bone for enough energy to maintain respiration.

But I've worked with hundreds—yes, thousands—of people who have experienced these sensations. A few of them are writing their own books. Most of them wanted to help their fellow victims. All of them expressed appreciation for the "Book of Life" which motivated me to become involved in their needs and offered them hope beyond the current condition.

I have not only preached concerning the problems of physical hunger, but also tried to bring people to the cross and to a response to God's cry for holiness, righteousness, and a closer walk with him. When I was leading the Youth for Christ Ministry, I used a phrase that applies to this subject on hunger. "Walk softly before the Lord." We have to walk softly before God and remain conscious of his leadership and presence all the time. It isn't easy, but it gets lasting results.

Over the years I've certainly learned that money doesn't make you happy. Most poor people don't know they're poor and are not a bit jealous of those of us who consider ourselves "rich." I don't find two-thirds-world people jealous of us in America. If anything, they may feel sorry for us. I've learned the Apostle Paul's comment that you can be content in whatever state you find yourself. But that doesn't mean you have to give up all hope, ambition, or motivation. Paul never gave up his struggle to get out of prison. Neither must we give up our struggle to make sure people have enough to feed their children and a place to bed them down for the night. Part of what God gives us today—with which we should be content— is a burning desire to improve our lot tomorrow through faith *and* works.

How I Cope

Here's how I cope with the burden of massive problems such as these: If I do everything I can then the problem is no longer mine. It's God's. And if I do everything I can, and you do everything you can, and we get everybody around us doing everything they can, then eventually it is no longer our problem. It belongs to God.

You and I, and all the hungry millions are invited to one final banquet. Not only will it celebrate the end of want, of suffering, and of death itself, it will celebrate the end of a gnawing hunger in the heart of God. No amount of food or wealth can by our way into the celebration. We must confirm our invitation through faith in our Lord Jesus Christ alone— but then obey through our work, and service, and love. Are you planning to come? I, along with millions of hungry people, sincerely hope so.

Notes

Chapter One

1. Arthur Simon, "Greed Keeps Third World Hungry," *Los Angeles Times,* March 2, 1988, Part II, p. 7.
2. Tom Sine, *The Mustard Seed Conspiracy,* (Waco, Texas: Word Books, 1981), p. 55.
3. Staff report, "Starvation Tactics in a Nasty Little War," *US News and World Report,* March 21, 1988, p. 11.
4. Jim Wallis, *Agenda for Biblical People,* (New York: Harper and Row, 1976), p. 85.
5. Ann Landers, *Los Angeles Times,* May 15, 1988, Part VI, p. 15.

Chapter Two

1. William and Paul Paddock, *Famine-1975,* (Boston: Little and Brown, 1967).
2. Norman Rohrer, *Open Arms,* (Wheaton, Illinois: Tyndale House, 1987), p.140.
3. "Remarks on Hunger at Denison University," U.S. Rep. Tony P. Hall, Ohio, Oct. 10, 1986.
4. Richard J. Barnet, *The Lean Years: Politics in the Age of Scarcity,* (New York: Simon & Schuster, 1980), p. 309.
5. Robert McAfee Brown, "Other Eyes, Other Voices," *A.D.*, February 1980, pp. 31-32.

Chapter Three

1. *Homeless in America,* edited by Michael A.W. Evans, (Washington D.C.: Acropolis Books and The National Mental Health Association, 1988).
2. Nancy Elliot, "Hard Times," *Newsweek,* March 21, 1988, p. 50.
3. Tom Mathews, "What Can Be Done," *Newsweek,* March 21, 1988, p. 57.
4. David Whitman, "America's Hidden Poor," *U.S. News and World Report,* Jan. 11, 1988, p. 19.
5. Ibid., p. 20.
6. Garry Abrams, "A Student of the Mean Streets," *Los Angeles Times,* Feb. 17, 1988, Part V, p. 2.
7. Ibid., p. 2.
8. Peter Marin, "How We Help and Harm the Homeless," *Utne Reader,* Jan./Feb. 1988, p. 40.
9. Constance F. Parvey, "Homeless Women: Priorities," *Christianity and Crisis,* March 16, 1987, p. 94.
10. Ramona Parish, "Messages from a Welfare Mom," *Newsweek,* May 23, 1988, p. 10.
11. Fred Muir, "Nattily Dressed Homeless Man Has a Mission," *Los Angeles Times,* Saturday, March 26, 1988, Part II, p. 3.
12. Marin, "How We Help and Harm the Homeless," p. 39.
13. Sine, *"The Mustard Seed Conspiracy,"* pp. 27-8.
14. "Remarks on Hunger at Denison University," U.S. Rep. Tony P. Hall. Ohio, Oct. 10, 1986.

Chapter Four

1. Sine, *The Mustard Seed Conspiracy,* p. 86.
2. Eloise Salholtz, "Morals Mine Field," *Newsweek,* October 23, 1986, p. 92.
3. Ibid., p. 92.
4. Steve Garber, "Going First Class on the Titanic," *Christianity Today,* November 20, 1987, p. 25.
5. Robert M. Bowman, Jr., "What's New in the New Religions?" *Moody,* November 1987, p. 69.
6. Ibid., p. 74.
7. Mike Yaconelli, "Becoming Pagan," published in *Wittenburg Door,* Aug-Nov., 1987, from back cover.
8. Sine, *The Mustard Seed Conspiracy,* p. 70.
9. Editors, "Secular vs. Christian Humanism," *Eternity,* January, 1982, p. 15.
10. Donald G. Bloesch, "Secular Humanism—Not the Only Enemy," *Eternity,* Jan. 1982, p. 22.
11. Sine, *The Mustard Seed Conspiracy,* p. 55.

Chapter Six

1. Emily T. Smith, "Stress: The Test Americans are Failing," *Business Week,* April 18, 1988, p. 76.
2. Kathleen Brady, "Simply To Be Normal," *Parade,* April 17, 1988, p. 14.
3. Ted Engstrom with Robert C. Larson, *Seizing the Torch,* (Ventura, California: Gospel Light Publications, 1988) p. 160.
4. Andrew Mollison, "Belief Climbing, But Church Attendance Is Falling," *Star-News,* July 16, 1988, B-6.
5. Ann Japenga, "Dropping Back In," *Los Angeles Times,* March 27, 1988, Part VI, p. 1.
6. Ibid., p. 1.

Chapter Seven

1. Merril F. Unger, *Unger's Bible Dictionary,* Chicago: Moody Press, Third Edition, 20th printing, 1974, p. 724.
2. Marin, "How We Help and Harm the Homeless," p. 37.
3. Rohrer, *Open Arms,* p. 143.
4. James Engel, "Engel Scale of Movement toward Christ," printed in *With Justice For All,* John Perkins, (Ventura, California: Regal Books, 1982), p. 137.
5. Perkins, *With Justice For All,* p. 50.
6. Rohrer, *Open Arms,* p. 126.
7. Ibid., p. 123.

Chapter Eight

1. Sine, *The Mustard Seed Conspiracy,* p. 154.
2. Francis O'Gorman, *Hillside Woman,* (Rio de Janero: Ecumencal Center for Action and Reflection, 1985) pp. 61, 95.
3. Jerry Buckley, "Bootstrap Time in a Luckless Land," *U.S. News & World Report,* Dec. 28, 1987/Jan. 4, 1988) pp. 88-91.
4. Ronald Brownstein, "On the Move with Richard Riordan, " *Los Angeles Times Magazine,* Aug. 21, 1988, p. 36.
5. Ibid., p. 18.
6. Staff writer, "I Accept in the Name of the Poor," *Time,* Oct. 29, 1979, p. 87.
7. Edmund G. Brown, Jr., "Passage to India," *Life,* April, 1988, pp. 29-32.
8. Ibid., p. 29.
9. Perkins, *With Justice For All,* pp. 155-6.

Chapter Nine

1. Steve Garber, "Going First Class on the Titanic," *Christianity Today,* November 20, 1987, p. 27.
2. Perkins, *With Justice For All,* pp. 52-54.
3. Rohrer, *Open Arms,* pp. 48-49.

Other Books of Interest from Servant Books

Knowing the Truth of God's Love
The One Thing We Can't Live Without
Peter Kreeft

Peter Kreeft has crafted a highly imaginative and thoughtful look at God's love that calls forth a heartfelt response to God as the Creator, Redeemer, and lover of our souls. He cuts through the divisive controversies of our day—including nuclear war and capital punishment—to demonstrate clearly why God's love is neither right nor left. *$8.95*

Knowing the Truth about the Resurrection
Our Response to the Empty Tomb
William L. Craig

Examining the evidence for the burial of Jesus, the empty tomb, the resurrection appearances, and the beginning of Christianity, William Craig demonstrates why the resurrection is the only answer that fits the facts. *$8.95*

Knowing the Truth about Heaven and Hell
Our Choices and Where They Lead Us
Harry Blamires

Harry Blamires believes that many people are in danger of forgetting the truth about heaven and hell— to their peril. He demonstrates with clarity why our choices have an immense impact on our eternal well-being *$8.95*

Available at your Christian bookstore or from:
**Servant Publications • Dept. 209 • P.O. Box 7455
Ann Arbor, Michigan 48107**
Please include payment plus $1.25 per book
for postage and handling.
*Send for our FREE catalog of Christian
books, music, and cassettes.*